SPACE PLANNING

Roberta Freifeld and Caryl Masyr
Framework for Information, Inc.

Special Libraries Association
Washington, DC

Cover Design by
Anita Winfield

Library of Congress Cataloging-in-Publication Data

    Space Planning/Framework for Information, Inc.
      p.   cm.
    ISBN 0-87111-356-2 $32.50
    1. Libraries—Space utilization.
    2. Libraries, Special.
    3. Library planning. I.Framework for Information, Inc. II.
Special Libraries Association
Z679.55.S58 1991
                 022.3—cc20   90-23269
                                            CIP

Contents

Acknowledgments

We would like to thank Honora Drohan for her contribution to the chapters on "Evaluating the Building," "Library Technology," and "Increasing Resource Sharing," and Pat Fairfield for indexing the finished text.

Introduction

THE GREATEST CHALLENGE facing organizations today is
lack of space: Everyone is running out of it. The information explosion, budget restrictions, the high cost of space, and expanding
collections have placed considerable burdens on libraries and
information centers.

In 1988, more than 300 billion pounds of paper were generated. Aside from original documents, other types of paper created
include photocopies, computer printouts, and hard copies of microfilm and microfiche. This translates into an overwhelming amount
of information on paper.

The cost of space is still high. Rent varies from $15 a square
foot in smaller cities, to $35-$45 in larger cities such as San Francisco, Los Angeles, and Boston, to as much as $50-$85 a square foot
in midtown New York City. These prices do not include additional
service costs such as cleaning, heating, electricity, and air conditioning, which may add another 20 percent to 50 percent to total space
costs. The high value of space is one reason for efficient space
management; *lack* of sufficient space is another.

No company has enough space nor does any company want to
pay for additional space. Most organizations do not want to pay for
information management at all because they do not see it as a
billable service or a revenue-generating operation. As a result,

companies do not deal with the need for space until the situation becomes a crisis.

Librarians understand the value of controlling information, but the average major corporation or law firm usually does not. The condition of most organizations' information systems is dismal. Therefore, librarians and information managers are faced with making the most out of existing space or justifying to management the need for additional space.

Because renovating a library or building a new one is costly, the finished structure must meet the needs of the whole organization. (See Figure I.1.)

Financial Considerations

Although changing a library environment is costly, management must understand that if the library does not change to meet its challenges, it will face even bigger renovation pressures and costs later.

Calculating project costs is essential. One way is to obtain detailed cost information from the contractor or vendor before signing the contract. Changes can be made in the contract if it appears that it might cost more than the allocated funds allow. Less expensive equipment might be substituted for the original order, or, as a last resort, the whole library design may have to be re-evaluated and reworked.

Librarians must know everything about the purchasing arrangement and know who has responsibility for following up on delivery times and arrangements. Although librarians might not get involved with the actual building contractor, they should know what the schedule is, whether it is being adhered to, how the different phases of the project will affect the facility's operation, and how this translates into money. For example, a library is being renovated and the schedule calls for work in the technical services area to begin on a certain date. The librarian has arranged for most of the technical services staff to take vacation or attend seminars during that week. The schedule is delayed for two weeks. What happens?

Develop a checklist of everything that needs to be done during the renovation. Before the job is approved, be sure to go through that list and determine that everything was completed satisfactorily.

ALTERNATIVES TO SPACE SHORTAGE

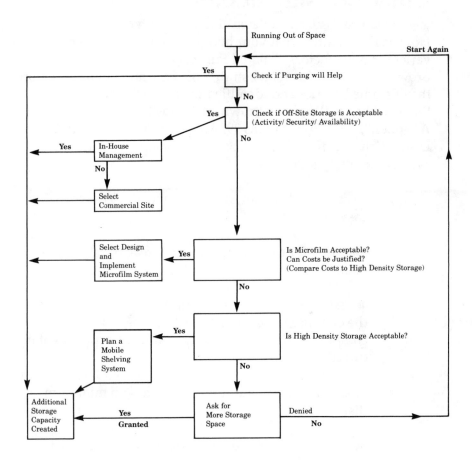

Figure I.1. Reprinted with permission of Greenwood Press, Inc.

Do not sign invoices for payment unless the work is done. Equipment is expensive, so make sure everything ordered is needed.

Other Considerations

Financial issues will determine your budget constraints. However, no matter what your budget, you must think about a variety of other factors. A noted European architect, H. Faulkner-Brown, conducted feasibility studies of space and buildings before they became libraries and identified ten criteria to be considered for the new library. (Faulkner-Brown, H., "Feasibility Studies before Adaption", IFLA Publications 39, Adaption of Buildings to Library Use", Michael Dewe, Ed., K.G. Saur, Munich, 1987, p. 17-45.) He says that a library should be:

1. *flexible*—with layout, structure, and services which are easy to adapt;

2. *compact*—for ease of movement of readers, staff, and books;

3. *accessible*—from the exterior into the building and from the entrance to all parts of the building, with an easy, comprehensible plan needing minimum supplementary directions;

4. *extendible*— to permit future growth with minimum disruption;

5. *varied*—in its provision of reader spaces, to give wide freedom of choice;

6. *organized*—to impose maximum confrontation between books and readers;

7. *comfortable*—to promote efficiency of use;

8. *constant in environment*—for the preservation of library materials;

9. *secure*—to control user behavior and loss of books; and

10. *economical*—to be built and maintained with minimal staff and financial resources.

Designing a library that is attractive, cost-effective, and user friendly involves numerous planning considerations. This book will address the following factors:

1. *Getting started*—what and how to measure the collection and the equipment in which it is housed.

2. *Evaluating the building*—considering floors, walls, ceilings, windows, columns or pillars, electrical systems, air-handling systems, and fire safety, and how they relate to the design of the library.

3. *Blueprints and floor plans*—a fast course on what factors to consider when laying out a library, and how to use blue-prints and floor plans in the design process.

4. *Equipment and furniture*—what types of shelving and furniture are best for your particular collection needs.

5. *Ergonomics*—the human factor; how work environments can affect productivity and morale.

6. *Technology*—what new technological products are avail-able and how they affect the library design.

7. *Resource sharing*—how to get the most resources with the least amount of space.

Chapter 1. Getting Started

BEFORE YOU CAN ACCURATELY DETERMINE how much space you will need, you must know how much collection housing you have, as well as how much and what types of material need to be accommodated. These procedures should be completed simultaneously. Such organization will help ensure that you do not count the same equipment twice.

Measuring the Collection Housing

Why do you need to measure the collection housing? It will allow you to determine how much space the equipment actually occupies on the floor—what computer people call "the footprint"— and to calculate how much material the housing you have can hold. You will need to pay attention to the latter point for equipment you plan to reuse and not supplement.

You must measure the outer and inner dimensions of each piece of equipment, that is, the height, width and depth of the equipment itself, and the width and depth of the inside of the file drawer or shelf. Measure each of the following:

1. Record the height, width, and depth of all shelving and the number of rows per shelving unit. Include any custom shelving built directly into the walls. Write down the manufacturer's name as well as the weight of the equipment when empty and full. This information will help you determine the floor load capacity, which will be discussed in Chapter 2.

2. Existing shelving will often be moved to the new location. Mark such equipment when developing floor plans. Use pressure-sensitive *removable* labels (or the labels will be there permanently). Avery and Dennison manufacture all kinds of labels including the pressure-sensitive removable kind. After labeling the shelving, cross-reference the unit to the floor plan.

3. Measure and count equipment in storage unless it will not be repaired or reused.

4. Count cabinets and pieces of furniture, especially collection housing for *nonbook formats*. Examples of nonbook storage include vertical files, newspaper files, cases for photographs, blueprints, microforms, film, CD-ROM, videotapes, and periodicals.

5. Measure each cabinet or case, regardless of its original use. For example, the microfilm collection may have expanded and overflowed into several shoeboxes, which you should measure and count.

6. Record the number, the type, and the description of file cabinets, such as four-drawer vertical or five-drawer lateral. Do the same for book stacks or bookcases, such as three- and seven-tier units. Do not assume that all equipment is the same size. For instance, some four-drawer vertical cabinets are 25 inches while others are 24 inches. Five-drawer verticals vary in size, too. Shelves also come in different sizes, and there may be custom shelves that were designed to fit certain areas.

7. Check drawers and shelves for disrepair and schedule repair for any equipment that will be reused. If you do not plan on repairing the equipment, make sure any damage will not affect the stored materials.

8. See if the cabinet or shelving unit locks. If so, where is the key? Does it work?

9. Know what the cabinet or shelving unit contains. Some units may not hold what you expect.

Measuring the Collection

Accurate collection measurements provide information for justifying the need for increased space and equipment. These measurements help you determine what will fit where and help you locate the collection on floor plans before and during a move, renovation, or redesign/reconfiguration.

For greatest accuracy, measure the linear inches (LI) of books actually housed on a particular shelf. Be sure to check circulation records for materials on loan so that they will be included. This method may be time-consuming; if you cannot measure the actual collection, use the shortcuts described later in this chapter. Whatever method you use, be sure to measure subcollections as well as the main one.

Measuring Subcollections

Measure subcollections separately because they often need special or separate housing located apart from the main collection. Examples of subcollections are uncataloged material, office collections, nonprint items, indexes and abstracts, vertical files, and rare books.

Uncataloged Material

Is this material to remain with the main collection? Be sure to indicate the method of arrangement, the material's condition, and a description of collection contents.

Office Collections

Some of these items are tools required for a job; others are personal favorites. Indicate the type of material and whether it is cataloged. Get this information from the occupant of the office involved.

Nonprint Items (Microforms, CD-ROM, Magnetic Media)

Accurate description is important here because equipment that houses one form of media may not be suitable for another. Note the contents and the arrangement of the material within the equipment as well as the actual measurement of the collection. Also indicate if special equipment to access the material is required: an example is a microform reader/printer.

Indexes and Abstracts

This material may occupy a single shelf or be spread out over many tables and shelves. Are prior years located in a separate place? If not, you may have to decide how many years of each title can be housed on tables. You can then send the rest into storage or house it on adjacent or back room shelves.

Periodical and Newspaper Display

Jot down the arrangement and manner of displaying this material.

Audio/Visual Collection

How full are the storage bins? What are the dimensions of each type of A/V material?

Vertical Files

Are files kept in regular or special file folders, and are these folders letter or legal size? Flag any full files that need to be broken down into smaller units. This is a good time to determine if new headings are needed or if unused files should be discarded.

Rare Books and Special Collections

Some special collections are housed away from the main collection; others are located near the reference desk. Check to see if the collection is housed in a section other than its regular call number sequence. In addition, look for under- or over-sized items, or material (such as maps) in nonstandard shapes.

Keep rare books in a separate location with temperature control, special preservation methods, and security. While conducting a title-by-title inventory, write down any unusual dimensions and special conditions of materials.

Alternative Collection Measurement Methods

When an actual shelf inventory and measurement is not possible due to time or financial constraints, consider a shelf list measure. In order to have an accurate count, you should have previously inventoried the material.

Measuring the Shelf List

This method works best in a large collection with an extensive shelf list. You will need to get the relative size of each call number range and then apply that ratio to the size of the whole collection. First measure the number of cards in the call number range. Estimate that one inch of cards equals 100 volumes, then calculate the number of volumes in each call number range. Industry standards are six to seven nonreference books per linear foot and five reference books per linear foot. Therefore, by dividing the total number of volumes by five, six, or seven (depending on what types of books are in the call number range), you can calculate the linear feet for each call number range.

To avoid frequent shifting of the collection after the move or expansion, estimate the space needed for each call number range now. Be sure to allow for growth and expansion. See the section on "Projecting Future Growth" below.

On-Line Measures

Most on-line circulation or cataloging systems give title and volume counts of holdings. But this method is not without problems. For instance, some software does not include a field for material format, so the user cannot tell from the entry if a particular item is, for example, a hardbound volume or in microform.

Serials present a similar problem. Titles are often entered under the name of the series, and the record may or may not include the number of volumes or parts of the single bibliographic record. For example, unless encyclopedias and certain law material are recorded as individual volumes in a circulation system, the only way to accurately measure the number of volumes is to count the entries on the shelf list card.

Projecting Future Growth

Determining the space required for future collection growth will enable the new space configuration to work. If you know how fast your collection is growing, use the book-per-linear-foot statistic to calculate how much future space to allocate for a given call number range. To determine how fast your collection is growing, identify the net number of items added to the collection during the past year and allow for at least that number annually. Ensure greater accuracy by identifying the net number of items added during the past five years. Then average that number.

Try to tie the anticipated growth to a specific call number sequence and media format. You can allow appropriate shelf space in that area to accommodate growth. Such planning will reduce backshifting as the collection increases. Also, since nonprint media are usually housed separately, you will want to know how much space to allow for the growth of these special collections.

One method of determining growth in a particular call number range is to relate the call number to a specific subject area in *The Bowker Annual,* which covers U.S. publishing output. Divide the number of new volumes added yearly to your unit in a specific subject area by the number *Bowker* lists as being published in that subject area during the year. Multiply the result by 100 for the percentage of publishing output to add during a year. Averaging over a five-year period will yield a more realistic figure.

Also use organizational or departmental financial information when estimating future growth. Has your collection budget increased or decreased from year to year? Do you expect major changes? The answers will give you an idea of the rate of future growth.

Accurately measuring the collection and its housing can be expensive and time-consuming, but completing these steps now can help you avoid surprises later. Doing measurements now will help you determine how items will be configured in the new space.

Chapter 2. Evaluating the Building

IF YOU HAVE NOT ALREADY DONE SO, you will now need to pay special attention to the building itself. Evaluating a building for its use or partial use as a library is becoming increasingly critical for librarians and architects. Less capital is available for building new structures; consequently, space originally designed for other purposes often must be used for a library.

Though type and size differences dictate various space usage requirements, all libraries have common design needs. Refer to H. Faulkner-Brown's ten criteria for libraries, which appear in the Introduction.

A proper evaluation of the prospective library space will cover both functional/technical and aesthetic considerations. Aesthetics, including lighting, appear in Chapter 3. In this Chapter we will cover such functional/technical issues as floor assessment (especially floor load capacity), walls, ceilings, windows, columns and pillars, electrical system, air-handling system, and fire safety considerations.

Floors

To understand floor load, librarians need to be aware of the concepts of *dead load* and *live load*. The weight of the building itself is the dead load—that which does not move and always remains the same. This includes elements such as steel, concrete, and wood that make up the building. The live load, on the other hand, is the weight of items or people that move or can be moved around the building. In a library, this includes books, equipment, supplies, fixtures, furniture, and people.

Believe it or not, too many people in one place at a given time can cause the building to collapse. When calculating load, the weight of these people must be separated from the other components of the live load. That is why, for example, the number of people allowed in a restaurant or auditorium may be limited.

High-Density Mobile Shelving

Floor load capacity is a major concern when high-density mobile shelving is used. Since this equipment can accommodate nearly double the volume of a conventional shelving system in the same area, the floor must be able to hold twice the load. This should not cause problems if the building originally housed heavy equipment, such as a factory or a garage, or if the floor has previously been reinforced.

Some interesting weight statistics for libraries were compiled from a variety of industry sources.

Paper weighs 58 pounds per cubic foot and a normal double-faced bookstack, 3 feet long, 20 inches deep (counting the width of the center poles and shelves), and 7 shelves high, weighs about 2,320 pounds fully loaded. The dimensions of the bookstack are very important, concerning fully weighted capacity. As the dimensions vary, so does the cubic volume. A double-faced stack with 8 shelves is much heavier than one with 7 shelves; one with 5 shelves is obviously much lighter.

If most stacks are estimated at about 85% full, the weight in the average book stack drops to 1,972 pounds. If an aisle size of 3 feet with an average 146 pounds per square foot is increased to 4 feet, the weight is redistributed at 120 pounds per square foot, the live-load rating for some library facilities.

By placing the stacks 8½ feet apart—10 feet center to center—the weight per square foot drops to 65.7 pounds. If the area is decreased and goes to compact shelving, where stacks stand about 2 feet apart center to center (counting one open aisle), the floor load is 329 pounds per square foot. Here the number of closed stacks in relation to the size of the one open aisle is critical.

What may happen when such loads are not considered? In one case, the architect involved in the development and design of a new library for a major corporation chose high-density mobile shelving for the library to maximize collection capacity and reduce square footage requirements. We asked about the floor load capacity of the area and whether a stress test had been performed. Had a structural engineer determined that the floor could support the weight of the equipment fully loaded with collection material? In response to our anxious questions, we were assured that no problems would arise.

Over $500,000 worth of high-density mobile shelving was installed in the library space on the building's 35th floor. Three weeks later, we received a frantic phone call. It seemed that because of a collapse, the 35th floor was soon to be on the 34th floor. This meant that the entire library collection had to be removed from its shelving, and all the shelving (including rails and flooring) dismantled, so that the floor could undergo structural strengthening.

Bolstering

That strengthening, known as bolstering, allows the building to support the additional weight. To understand the process, one must be aware of a basic construction principle.

Major components of a building's superstructure are the girders and beams that tie the floors and wall together. Concrete poured over a metal pan is the usual filler between the girders and beams. The method of reinforcing the floor is fairly standard: The ceiling is removed from the floor below and the filler area is reduced by adding more beams. Another floor is then constructed several inches above the original floor and these reinforcements are connected to the building's superstructure. Because reinforcements add to the building's dead load, it must be determined if other tenants have also strengthened their floors. In addition, the *vertical* columns of the building need to be able to carry this added weight. A structural engineer can provide more information on these topics.

Walls

In evaluating the building, consider the current and expected future use of walls and wall space. Some walls are movable and should be calculated as part of the live load. Some are solid. Other walls house the building's heating and wiring systems. Still other walls may not offer hanging space because of such permanent attachments as pipes.

The material the wall is composed of will tell you how to hang supporting shelves, bookcases, and other wall-hung items. This, in turn, has weight implications. Many pre-World War II buildings used pressboard for interior walls. Attaching angle braces to pressboard and sheetrock requires special hanging devices that may have a limited load-bearing capacity.

When you need to fasten heavy items to a wall, use the wall studs. A magnet will help you locate the nails that hold the walls to the studs. You also may want to use an electronic device called "The Stud Finder" available in home and building improvement stores. Remember that most studs are either twelve or eighteen inches apart, center to center. Mark stud locations on your floor plans for future reference.

Ceilings

What is the height of the facility's ceiling? Ceiling height in public or patron areas should be ten feet, while eight-foot-high ceilings work in staff areas. High ceilings mean greater noise level, as well as increased heating and cooling costs. Low ceilings have disadvantages, too: ceilings lower than eight feet limit shelving options. Lighting glare may also become a problem.

Does the space (or will it) have ceiling sprinkler installation? If so, you must, according to fire codes, leave an eighteen-inch clearance between sprinkler-head bottoms and shelving tops. This means that tier stacks that are 88$\frac{1}{4}$ inches high would require a minimum 8-foot, 10$\frac{1}{4}$-inch ceiling to comply with fire code regulations. If 8-foot, 10$\frac{1}{4}$-inch to 9-foot ceilings are unrealistic, sprinklers could be installed parallel in the ceiling between rows of stacks to comply with regulations. For further information, contact your local fire department. If sprinklers are not an issue, still leave adequate clearance to promote air circulation and allow for changing or repairing light fixtures. Three to seven inches is usually adequate in such cases.

Windows

Windows interrupt continuous wall space and affect a building's lighting and heating requirements. On the human side, windows enhance the environment and provide more comfortable space for patrons, provided the interior design of the building uses the windows advantageously. Because northern exposures provide indirect sunlight, they are ideal for libraries.

When doing your building study, gather information on window measurements, composition, location, and so on. Do the windows open? If so, how? Also include locations and characteristics of skylights and plate-glass walls. Blocking off skylights with stacks or furniture can create fresh air problems in the rest of the library.

Columns and Pillars

Columns and pillars serve a variety of functions: they may be a load-bearing structural support, a decoration, or a conduit for wiring and air handling systems. The location of columns affects layout, space, visibility, and security. You can have decorative columns removed, but those used for support or wiring are permanent. Some people learn this the hard way. In one situation, the architect insisted that newly purchased space-saving equipment could be efficiently configured by removing an abutment in one wall to accommodate an additional shelving unit. This abutment was, in fact, an electrical closet and, of course, remained in the organization longer than the architect did.

Electrical System

Electrical power also affects space layout and configuration. Gather information on circuits, switch locations, plugs, outlets, electrical closets, and so on. (For detailed information on lighting

Figure 2.1. Columns, Louisiana State University Library. Photograph courtesy of Metropolitan Business Systems, Inc.

see Chapter 5.) Mark switches, circuits, and outlets on your floor plan.

Wisely allocating power prevents fires, service interruptions, and computer crashes. When manual systems are automated, dedicated lines (electrical lines having no other equipment or outlets sharing the power source) must be used. For computer equipment, invest in a true uninterruptible power system (U.P.S.) that will handle the total voltage of all computer terminals. This affords fewer data errors, protection from lightning, and reduced down-time. It also dramatically lowers service expenses and prolongs equipment life.

Avoid rewiring expenses by placing photocopiers, computers, and other electrical equipment next to outlets. As you plan, consult professional electrical engineers and electricians. This is not a job for amateurs.

Air Handling

Though lighting is covered in Chapter 5, you need to consider lighting/air-handling relationships early in the space planning process. Many lighting fixtures can be installed as part of the heating, ventilating, and air-conditioning system. Air may circulate through special holes in or around the light fixtures. Some fixtures have holes at either end. Paneled fixtures have small cracks around the periphery to do the same thing. In ceiling systems (a prefabricated ceiling assembled on the job), a barely noticeable crack among the acoustical tiles may handle the air and may only involve the lighting fixtures indirectly.

It is a good idea to make the lighting system a part of the overall heating/ventilating/air-conditioning system, although special circumstances may require otherwise. All electricity consumed can be directly translated into heat. If allowed to accumulate, heat can interfere with the air-conditioning system and even blow fuses.

Why waste heat in this energy-conserving age? Why not reuse it? Several libraries have done just that. The buildings are primarily heated and cooled by the waste heat generated by electrical equipment, such as the lights, and the body heat of persons using the facility.

Fire Safety

National, state, local, and insurance company fire safety codes also affect space allocation. The National Fire Protection Association Life Safety Code specifies 200 feet as the maximum travel distance from any point to any exit if the building has no sprinkler system, and 300 feet if the building has one. Dead-end corridors cannot exceed fifty feet; large libraries must have more than one major door, although the other door may be an alarmed one-way exit. Open access to fire doors may be required for libraries in large office buildings. The code specifies that the second exit must be located as far as possible from the first one.

For more information about fire codes for your particular area, write the National Fire Protection Association, Batterymarch Park, P.O. Box 9101, Quincy, MA 02269-9101, or call (617) 770-3500. If you work in an earthquake-prone area, your library may also have to comply with earthquake codes. The aforementioned organization has information about those codes as well.

Design characteristics such as floors, ceilings, windows, and structural elements (e.g., pillars and columns) all play an important role in determining whether a building can, in fact, be used as a library. Once this decision is made, the creative task of designing the space begins.

Chapter 3. Layout of the Special Library: Blueprints and Floor Plans

SPACE PLANNING IS NOT simply a matter of square feet, equipment, and furniture. It is essential to consider psychological factors as well as technical and space issues. In addition, library traffic patterns and work flow must be included in the layout.

The arrangement of book stacks, equipment, workstations, and furniture affects the efficiency of work and the available space. Time and energy may be wasted if staff has to go too far to get to needed materials, or if staff frequently has to leave workstations. Thus, the layout of the equipment and furniture, library collection materials, people, traffic patterns, work flow, lighting, acoustics, and even the color and decor of the library, greatly affect the way staff and users function in the library.

Irene Place and Estelle Popham, in their book *Information and Records Management* (Englewood Cliffs, NJ: Prentice Hall, 1966, p. 213), state: "Good layout is the conquest of inner space. It considers available office space, arrangement of library equipment, furniture and reference areas, work stations, environment, work flow, and the principles of motion economy."

It is not necessary to be a professional space planner to lay out a library. Library equipment and furniture vendors, architects, consultants, and space design specialists can help to develop the optimum layout. Just get the facts, study them, consult the proper people, and draw the plan. Use a tape measure to measure the exact space available. How long and wide is it? Where are the doors and windows? Where are columns and struts which affect placement of equipment and furniture? Where are the electrical outlets? Make a list of things that will be used in the area. Draw an exact diagram. Show the direction in which the doors swing because doors that swing into a room affect the location of things near room entrances. How many bookshelves and work stations are there?

Libraries are equipment- and furniture-intensive. To maximize efficiency and effectiveness, the library should be attractive, usable, and comfortable. If not, it will undermine its main purpose, which is to enable users and staff to function at peak efficiency, locate needed materials quickly, and concentrate on referencing materials with a minimum of interruption and noise.

To renovate an existing library, conduct an inventory of equipment and furniture. This will show current inventory that must be included on the floor plans, which inventory can be discarded, what new equipment and furniture must be purchased, and the measurements of new equipment and furniture that can be accommodated in the space. See Chapter 1 for details on measuring your collection and collection housing.

Five major elements are involved in planning a library. They are:

1. Collection space for book stacks, file equipment, or shelving; microfilm and microfiche storage equipment; and newspaper and journal storage and display equipment;

2. Staff space for work stations, technical processing areas, reference desks, and circulation desks;

3. User space for reviewing-area carrels and chairs, lounges, and microfilm/microfiche reader/printer work stations and chairs;

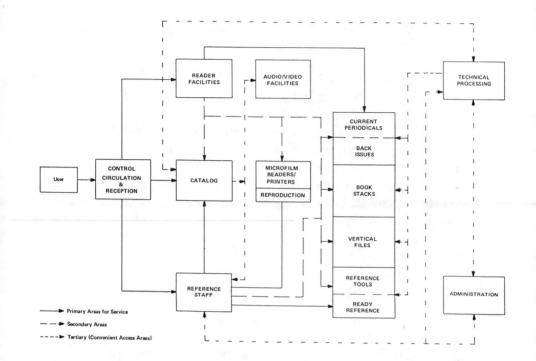

Figure 3.1. Reprinted with permission of Special Libraries Association © 1972.

4.   Internal circulation and traffic flow within the library, which translates into easy access to materials, staff, equipment, and furniture; and

5.   Space for support functions, such as photocopying machines and mail handling.

Collection space is the top priority. Books, periodicals, hard copy files, and materials in all media formats (e.g., CD-ROM, microfilm, and microfiche) are the reasons the special library exists. The collection is the core of the library and must be given sufficient space for current requirements, as well as for future growth and expansion. After that, consider user and staff space requirements.

Furniture and equipment layouts are not easy for the inexperienced space planner. However, it is essential that the space planner consider the building structure, floor load capacity (live and distributed load factors), available usable space, and individual user and staff needs and requirements.

Collection Space

First, determine linear shelving requirements. These measurements are then translated into shelving equipment square footage dimensions which must be drawn exactly to size on the floor plans. To estimate correctly, measure the books and other media to be housed in the library in linear inches or linear feet. In addition, know the number of library staff members and the number of library users at peak, normal, and off times.

The number of books per square foot depends not only on the sizes of the books, but also on the size of book stacks and bookcases; height of book stacks and bookcases (i.e., the number of tiers/shelves per bookstack or bookcase); depth of shelves; length of ranges (i.e., width of units/sections and number of units/sections per row which make up a range; and widths of aisles between ranges. Remember, double-faced ranges (i.e., book ranges that are placed back-to-back) will require less aisle space.

Determine the number of books per linear inch or foot, using industry standards or random sampling of shelves. Then, convert linear inches (LI) or linear feet (LF) into the number of shelving units, or into square footage requirements by the following method:

1. Determine the height of the library's ceiling. Building fire code regulations require an eighteen-inch clearance between the tops of shelving and the bottoms of sprinkler heads when there is a ceiling sprinkler system installation. If there are no sprinklers, enough room must be allowed between the tops of shelving and the ceiling to permit the flow of air and, when necessary, the opening of casements.

2. Once the ceiling height, the existence of an overhead sprinkler, and any floor loading limitations are known, the planner can determine the height of the shelving. The planner can also determine the number of shelves per shelving section and the number of shelving sections.

3. Measuring the distance between columns and other obstructions in an area will provide the length available for shelving ranges. For example, assuming no additional space must be allocated for obstructions in either wall or within the area, 6 feet allows the use of two 36-inch-wide single-faced book units or one 48-inch and one 24-inch, single-faced unit. A 9-foot ceiling (108 inches), with no overhead sprinkler installation, means that 97 ¼-inch-high units can be used. This would allow seven tiers per unit, or six tiers if oversized books higher than twelve inches are housed.

4. Determine the number of linear inches or feet of shelving in each section, i.e., the number of shelves per section multiplied by the linear inches or feet per shelf, minus one to two inches per shelf for clearance space.

5. A seven-tier, 36-inch wide unit/section would afford 34 to 35 inches per tier, or a total of 238-245 LI per unit. This is because one should always allow 1 to 2 inches of clearance per shelf to facilitate access and retrieval of books,

prevent wear and tear on books and fingers, and preserve the lives of bindings.

6. Knowing the current LI or LF of the library collection and the projected net growth rate, the number of tiers per shelving unit, and the LI or LF per shelving unit, determine how many units are necessary to house the current book collection and to provide space for growth and expansion.

Remember that when calculating the number of units, double-faced stacks should be counted as two separate units. If standard twelve-inch bookcases or bookshelf depths are used, the square footage is easily computed. The depth and width per unit are multiplied by the number of units. Then, assuming 30 to 36-inch-wide aisles in between shelving ranges or for ranges sharing an aisle, the total square footage required can be calculated by multiplying aisle width by length of shelving range.

Running short ranges is wasteful. Running single-faced stacks around the library's wall also reduces the collection volume count. Wall space should be used instead for people/traffic flow. In addition to being expensive, single-faced stacks are not space efficient. Use double-faced stacks whenever possible.

If a 10 percent per year collection growth rate is calculated, a library with 3,000 usable square feet for collection housing would require an extra 6,000 square feet in twenty years, or a total of 9,000 square feet. Adding a 6 percent configuration loss would mean that, in twenty years, the collection would need 9,540 square feet. A configuration loss is added because the area probably will have some nonassignable space and will not be a perfect square or rectangle.

Aaron Cohen and Elaine Cohen, in their book *Designing and Space Planning For Libraries: A Behavioral Guide* (New York: R. R. Bowkev, 1979, p. 66-67), comment that: "Nonassignable space is space that can't be used for library purposes—corridors, stairwells, elevators, rest rooms, mechanical rooms and such. Nonassignable space also implies nonusable nooks and crannies... It is best to keep it to a minimum—no more than 25 percent. Too much nonassignable space translates into lack of control and may also necessitate additional staff members—besides excessive walking."

For calculation purposes, assume a minimum of 6 percent and average 10 percent configuration loss. However, if the building has substantial nonassignable space or is circular, the configuration loss can be as high as 25 percent.

Standards

Space requirements for staff areas are difficult to generalize. Some studies indicate that fifty to sixty square feet for each clerical employee is adequate. This provides for a fifty-four-inch desk, chair, file cabinet, and aisle space. However, because of the high space costs in some large cities, actual in-use standards may be as low as forty square feet per clerical worker. Theoretically, space requirements increase as you go up the management ladder. For example, a supervisor would have 100 to 125 square feet; department manager, 200 to 300 square feet; and chief librarian/library director, 400 to 450 square feet. Again, actual square footage is often lower in large cities because of high space costs.

Allow space in which personnel can move about and use furniture and equipment. The amount of space needed depends on the shelving and file equipment used, as well as how often staff and users access the material.

Staff members' workstations must be placed and translated into exact measurements so that desks, file cabinets, chairs, and book trucks can be drawn correctly on floor plans. Estimate the areas required by staff using the forty to sixty square foot per person standards for clerical workers. Also consider shared equipment such as photocopiers, microfilm or microfiche reader/printers, card catalogs, and book trucks. Be sure to allocate space for office supplies and special functions such as binding. Remember to allow space for bathrooms, lounges, a kitchen, a circulation desk, book trucks, and a loading dock.

User Space

Library traffic statistics will tell how many user seats are needed. Pull-out reference shelves allow users to review material at the book stacks and may decrease the number of seats and user

Figure 3.2. Back office work area. Library of a large New York law firm.

Figure 3.3. Reading area furniture, Southern Baptist Hospital Library. Photograph courtesy of Metropolitan Business Systems, Inc.

reviewing areas and carrels needed. Check any state or organizational standards that might mandate the number of seats per person.

The type and size of chairs have an impact on the amount of space required. Obviously, armchairs take up more space than chairs without arms.

Too much working space can be as serious a problem as not enough space. Be sure to allow enough space, but do not waste it. (See Appendix 4 for industry space planning standards.)

When planning space requirements for the special library, remember these important points:

1. The layout should be flexible.

2. One large area is preferable to an equivalent area of small rooms because a single area permits better lighting, ventilation, supervision, and communication.

3. Dominant work flows and communication needs should be given the highest priorities.

4. Central service functions like reference work and special equipment should be located conveniently near the departments and personnel whom they service most.

5. Provision should be made for peak load rather than for off-time requirements. Use statistics for past annual volume of work as the basis for planning future requirements.

6. Standard space guidelines should be adhered to in planning and allocating space. Where maximum and minimum standards have been set, maximum standards provide for expansion and usually increase efficiency.

7. Such heavy equipment as photocopiers, file cabinets, and shelving (book stacks) should be positioned only where floor load capacity is sufficient to bear the weight.

8. Adequate floor-based electrical outlets should be provided for computers and typewriters. Wall outlets should also be provided.

9. Bookshelves and file equipment can be used to create corners, aisles, counters, or room dividers. However, this secondary purpose should not disrupt the primary function of housing the collection.

10. Know which way a door swings to prevent placing equipment in its path.

Floor Plans and Blueprints

A floor plan is an architectural scale drawing, showing the size and arrangement of rooms, halls, equipment, and other items on one floor of a building. A blueprint is a photographic reproduction of architectural or engineering plans in black or white on a blue background.

Two excellent textbooks on blueprint reading and drawing are: Hooper, Donald R. *Blueprint Reading Made Easy.* Rev. ed., New York: Dreyfus, 1983, and Lightle, R. Paul. *Blueprint Reading and Sketching.* New York: McKnight, 1983 (out of print).

The first step in a space plan or layout is acquiring and studying a recent and accurate floor plan, blueprint, or architectural drawing of the space. Get plans from architects, building engineers, maintenance firms, or building inspectors. Remember that separate plans are drawn up for plumbing, wiring, furniture, air-handling systems, flooring, carpentry, walls, windows, and other structures.

Floor Plans

Essential plans are those that include accurate markings of permanent physical characteristics, such as walls, columns, pillars, struts, floors, and windows. The condition and accuracy of these plans will vary. The plans should be measured and double-checked for accuracy. The legend explains the scale which is generally either $\frac{1}{8}$ inch = 1 foot or $\frac{1}{4}$ inch = 1 foot. Occasionally a legend will say $\frac{1}{16}$ inch = 1 foot, but this is really too small to use. Measure doors.

Because the standard door is 3 feet wide, the planner can determine or verify the scale of the floor plan from this measurement.

Blowups of floor plans can be made on photocopiers. For example, the planner might want to enlarge a $\frac{1}{16}$-inch scale floor plan to a $\frac{1}{8}$-inch or $\frac{1}{4}$-inch scale, or a $\frac{1}{8}$-inch scale floor plan to a $\frac{1}{4}$-inch scale. However, the photocopier can distort the new scale, so check for accuracy. Better yet, to guarantee the correct scale, use a photocopier designed for floor plans or one which produces accurate scales for copies and reduces and enlarges to exact scale. Make many copies so that you can create different versions.

Drawing floor plans using a $\frac{1}{4}$-inch scale is best because a $\frac{1}{8}$-inch scale is too small, harder to work with, and more apt to cause errors. A $\frac{1}{16}$-inch scale is the most difficult to work with and almost always leads to errors.

Pace off the room size, door placements, columns, windows, and walls using a tape measure, and compare these measurements with the floor plans or blueprints for accuracy.

Computer-aided design (CAD) software can speed up the space planning process. However, if that is too expensive, use templates, tracing paper, and graph paper (either $\frac{1}{4}$-inch or $\frac{1}{8}$-inch scale) to produce cutouts which can be moved around on the blueprint. Several helpful office planning kits are also available. An excellent one is the Plan-a-Flex Office Design Kit by Stanley Tools in New Britain, Connecticut. It includes equipment symbols (even high-density mobile shelving symbols) and a ruled grid board. Another kit on the market is Peel.N.Plan Templates, manufactured in Laguna Hills, California.

Blueprints

If original blueprints are not available, use reductions or photocopies. If original blueprints are available, make working copies. Place the tracing paper over the library areas on the blueprint and trace these areas. Then photocopy the original blueprint. Make sure that the photocopies are not enlarged or reduced by placing the traced area over the photocopy and verifying that the scale is still correct.

If blueprints are filled in already, photocopy the tracing paper outline. Then cut and paste the photocopies over the original blueprint, and photocopy this version. Once again, place the original tracing paper outline over the final photocopy to ensure that the scale is still correct. Or, use correction fluid for photocopies instead of putting the photocopied traced outline on the already filled in area.

Templates

Templates are predrawn equipment and furniture replicas which can be moved around on the floor plan to evaluate possible arrangements. Art supply stores sell plastic templates that feature the most common outlines for furniture and equipment. They come in ¼-inch and ⅛-inch scale models.

Templates are easy to create. Most furniture manufacturers supply scales of their product lines with which to draw templates. Templates can be fashioned from graph paper, mylar, or other materials, or you can make a three-dimensional cardboard model for a quick overview of a layout that is helpful in explaining the design to others.

Graph paper makes calculations easier. Every ¼" or ⅛" on graph paper equals one foot. Make certain that the scale of the graph paper and the scale of the blueprint or floor plan are the same.

Once a set of templates has been made for all equipment, photocopy these designs and cut them out for use in multiple layouts. This eliminates redrawing the templates for each new layout, or worse, settling for only one layout. Having several different layouts allows time to reflect and let others review the designs and assist in the decision process. It helps to paste the templates on cardboard before cutting them out. This gives the templates more durability and body, and makes it easier to hold and move them around.

CAD Software

There are a number of low-priced, easy-to-use computer-assisted-design software packages available to run on personal computers with color monitors and graphics boards. CAD software allows the creation of detailed, professional-quality floor plans or architectural drawings. It allows the designer to create, revise, detail, calculate dimension, and plot floor plans without the time

Figure 3.4. Reading area furniture, Louisiana State University Library. Photograph courtesy of Metropolitan Business Systems, Inc.

Figure 3.5. Reception area furniture, Southern Baptist Hospital
Library. Photograph courtesy of Metropolitan Business Systems,
Inc.

and effort that manual drafting requires. This fast and flexible software facilitates the production of architectural and engineering drawings and enables the creation of different layouts without redrawing equipment, furniture, and other items for each version.

Some of the better software packages are: EasyCAD, Generic CAD, Drafix 1 Plus/Drafix CAD Ultra, Versacad, LaserCAD, DesignCAD, and CADVANCE. AutoCAD is more difficult to learn and use, but gives the most professional product. (See Appendix 5 for vendor information.)

Layout and Design

Heavy traffic areas and areas housing the book collection (bookcases/stacks) should be designed as squares or rectangles because these shapes are the easiest to work with and the most flexible. Because file cabinets and bookcases and stacks are essentially rectangular, they fit better when placed inside a square or rectangular area. Equipment can be run from either north to south or east to west.

In addition to the acoustic and lighting benefits of a square area, there is less walking involved because all points are equidistant from the center. In addition, a square affords centralization and control because all areas within the square can be seen from the center.

If a completely square or rectangular library is not possible, Cohen and Cohen advocate the concept of "the central square." The authors suggest "the central square" for areas with the heaviest user activity because these areas require the most control or supervision. Staff areas, operations, and meeting rooms that require privacy and less noise should not be placed in the central square. As the authors say: "The central square area should be the focal point of the library from which all user activities radiate, an open place where people and activities converge." (Cohen and Cohen, 1979, p. 68-69)

Placing stairs and elevators next to each other is an effective use of space. In multilevel libraries, stairs and elevators relate and so should all entrances and exits. In addition, place corridors and walkways that run throughout the library near the departments that use the library most frequently. If there is more than one entrance or exit, each one should be placed closest to the department it serves.

In a multilevel library, the main entrance/exit should be located on the first floor in the most important user area. The first floor also should contain the most important user services.

It is important to determine those services that are used most and how they relate to each other in terms of library space. Services which are expected to grow faster than others should receive more space. Services that might be reduced or eliminated in the future should be considered. This information will help the planner relate areas in the library to each other so that the library operates as efficiently as possible. Back office operations such as technical services (cataloging, book processing), boxing books for interlibrary loan and storage, receiving messengers, and staging and facilitating areas should not be the first function the users see. These services should be in less accessible areas, but still near doors (not the main entrance) to facilitate the flow of materials to and from the library.

Access

Accessibility is important for all libraries. If a library is not accessible or delivery service is not efficient, departments may hoard books or use other sources for information. On the other hand, materials should not be too accessible. Unauthorized personnel should not be permitted to go directly to the book stacks or reference collection. Arrange these areas so that access is controlled.

Shortening aisle widths increases existing collection space. Added space, better collection security, fewer damaged books, and decreased shelf reading time are some advantages to closed stacks. However, disadvantages include decreased browsing capability, longer staff retrieval time, and more complex recordkeeping procedures.

Agreement

After needed space is estimated for the collection, users, staff, furniture, equipment, and aisles, make a scale layout drawing of every piece of furniture and equipment, with dotted lines showing work flow. By using layout drawings and templates, reconcile what exists with what is needed. Remember to allow adequate space for working areas and aisles.

Lastly, reconcile drawn layouts with the actual usable space and make figures accurate by breaking down each area in the library. Emphasize work flow, and functional arrangements of equipment, workstations, and furniture, including special areas that do not appear under staff, user, or collection areas (e.g., special rooms for presentations or meetings). Compare these again with the layouts to make sure the entire interior has been dealt with accurately and nothing has been ignored.

Do not panic by trying to remember space allowances and rules of space planning. Do sample layouts, move templates around on the floor plans, and then see if the arrangements comply with recommended standards. (See Appendix 4 for a listing of industry recommended space planning standards.)

Although space cannot be created where none exists, it can be maximized by proper planning and design.

Chapter 4. Furniture and Equipment Selection

SPECIAL NEEDS AND USES should be considered when selecting furniture for the electronic special library. Recommended table and chair heights are different for a computer than those recommended for reading or checking books and periodicals.

Provide furniture for patron as well as staff areas. Patron areas include reading and research rooms and rooms containing specialized equipment such as microform readers/printers, computers, and card or book catalogs (if not on-line).

Evaluate furniture for durability, flexibility, comfort, and efficiency, and for its intended use.

Chairs

Chairs are manufactured in materials such as wood, plastic, metal, or a combination of materials. Although not as easy to obtain as they once were, all-wood chairs are the most durable and comfortable. Use the right style of chair: reading chairs should be used for reading areas, and computer chairs for computer rooms.

The Bank of England chair is the most comfortable, durable, and economical, as well as the safest of any chair designed for library use. It is usually made of maple or oak. It was described as "the most comfortable chair on earth" by Professor Diana Vincent-Daviss, law librarian at the New York University School of Law.

Tables

A table must be measured, marked, and placed carefully on a layout, or it will be too short, too wide, or too long for its new location. The multiple uses of tables allow them to blend in with other furnishings, making them easily missed during the space evaluation process. Tables are used often as microcomputer stations and for microform readers.

Extra tables are useful during a space-implementation project. They can be used as stations for the handouts, as temporary circulation areas, and as places for workers. Each table used during the project should be marked with its final destination.

Each table should have a furniture record that notes its condition, composition, shape, manufacturer, size, and seating capacity. Measure and itemize tables and include notes about their construction, size, and such special features as extra legs, removable or addable dividers, and double widths. An extra-wide table can be separated only if the additional legs are available.

A table may work well in its present floor location because the space had the right bumps and carpet waves to keep it stable, or because the table uses a column as its fourth leg. Some high quality library furniture does not have adjustable or leveling legs, so, by default, its current location may be the best.

Micrographic readers/printers can be placed on carrels or several readers/printers can be arranged on a large table. The latter arrangement is usually preferable because traditional carrels are generally too small to accommodate the reader/printer and also allow enough work space for the patron. Large carrels can be purchased for readers/printers, but they are more expensive than regular-sized carrels.

Carrels, desks, and tables can be used for some computer equipment. However, if the computer includes a drive for CD-ROM or other optical disk applications, the work surface must be at least one foot wider than standard widths to accommodate the equipment.

Figure 4.1. Table. Library of a large law firm.

Figure 4.2. User table, Varnum & Riddering Library. Photograph courtesy of Metropolitan Business Systems, Inc.

Carrels

Carrels can be less space efficient than tables. However, carrels are appropriate in most special library situations where patrons desire privacy. They are generally more functional than tables because they have many uses such as computing, typing, viewing microforms and videotapes, listening to audiotapes, and using calculators. Carrels can be wired to accommodate all of these activities. In addition, carrels can have individual lights, telephones, and overhead shelves for books.

A carrel's work surface should be at least twenty-four inches deep by thirty-six inches wide. However, larger surfaces should be provided for computer and microform equipment. Because special libraries will be using more and more electronic equipment, designers and planners should purchase the oversized carrels.

Desks

Staff will use desks for technical services, circulation, and reference. Use standard secretarial desks for staff with clerical duties. For other staff, two-pedestal desks work well. Two-pedestal desks have drawers on both sides of the well, with pull-out writing shelves in each pedestal. The desk surface should be at least sixty inches wide and approximately thirty inches deep. A desk-back unit can provide additional storage space at the rear of the desk. This unit also will give privacy to the desk's occupant.

Wooden desks are usually purchased for reference, circulation, and executive personnel. If wooden desks are used heavily, they should have high-pressure laminate tops or Lucite glass covers. Service desks are usually designed with built-in protection for the surface.

A circulation desk is usually manufactured in modules, with each component serving a separate circulation function. These components can include discharge, charging machine, workstation, typing, open port, and corner units, as well as vertical files and book chutes. The units can be purchased individually and configured to meet the special needs of each library. Like desks, the surface of the circulation desk should be protected with a laminate, Lucite, glass, or other wear-resistant material.

Modular Workstations/Work Units

Many manufacturers, for example, Steel Case, Tab Products, and Herman Miller, make excellent modular workstations and units that afford great space savings. Many of these also have overhead and under-table storage units for greater storage capacity.

Equipment

Library collections can be housed in an almost endless variety of equipment, ranging from standard shelving to push-button, high-density mobile shelving. Equipment should be chosen for its serviceability and suitability for the material to be housed.

In the past, nearly all library materials were books and other paper-based resources, e.g., indexes, abstracts, periodicals, and newspapers. Today, the library must keep many different types of material to provide the most up-to-date and comprehensive information to its patrons. New equipment is needed to hold microforms, computer printouts, magnetic and optical media, and audio and video equipment.

However, the special library still needs to provide equipment for traditional library materials such as books, newspapers, and periodicals. Also, be sure to provide equipment for a rare book collection or for displaying art objects or other nonbook material. Electronic resources will continue to grow, but it is doubtful they will ever completely replace paper-based materials.

Shelving

There are many shelving options for libraries; selection of equipment depends on the use of the materials on the shelves. Standard wooden and steel shelving of the bracket type are used most commonly for active materials to which patrons have access. Steel warehouse shelving can be used in closed-access collections. Although a section of warehouse shelving occupies more floor space than a double-faced section of library shelving, it actually has more storage space because books are stored three or four deep on each shelf.

Figure 4.3. Carrel, Western Theological Seminary Library. Photograph courtesy of Metropolitan Business Systems, Inc.

Figure 4.4. Carrel, library of a large law firm.

Figure 4.5. Reference desk, Bonneville Power Administrative Engineering Library. Photograph courtesy of Metropolitan Business Systems, Inc.

Figure 4.6. Circulation desk, Muskegon High School Library. Photograph courtesy of Metropolitan Business Systems, Inc.

Figure 4.7. Modular workstation with overhead storage. Photograph courtesy of Metropolitan Business Systems, Inc.

For open-access collections, wooden shelving is generally used in such high-visibility areas as reference and circulation. Special-purpose or custom-designed shelving is manufactured more easily in wood than in metal. However, wooden library shelves are the most expensive type of library shelving.

Metal shelves are less expensive and come in three types: storage or warehouse shelves, slotted or standard shelves, and bracket-type shelves. Libraries use bracket shelves more than the other type because they are stable and come in many heights and shelf depths.

Bookstack end panels can be easily cleaned and wear better than metal. Expensive end panels for less costly stacks create a look of richness and coordinate with the library's decor. Steel stacks can be ordered in colors other than grey and sand, or can be refinished using a process called electrostatic painting, which sprays on new color. Stacks can also be purchased with built-in lighting, or individual lighting can be provided for separate aisles. Lighting every other shelving range is less expensive.

Mobile Shelving

Use of high-density mobile shelving (compact shelving) should be seriously considered by planners of the new library. Such shelving can often double the storage space of conventional equipment. It also requires fewer permanent aisles, increases security, and protects materials from exposure to light, dirt, and moisture. It is generally used for closed-access stacks.

High-density storage equipment uses mechanical methods to increase storage capacity. There are three different high-density storage systems: rotary file units where carriers rotate vertically or horizontally, like the Lektriever and Remstar systems; center column equipment; and mobile shelving.

Mobile shelving offers the greatest storage capacity. There are two different types of high-density mobile shelving: lateral and vertical. With both types, rails are built into the floor or a sub-floor so that sections can be moved. This reduces the number of aisles between shelves because the sections can be moved to allow access to needed files.

With lateral mobile shelving, two or three shelving rows are placed in back of each other without aisles in between them. To

Figure 4.8. Newspaper storage, library of a large law firm.

Figure 4.9. Periodicals storage, Muskegon High School Library. Photograph courtesy of Metropolitan Business Systems, Inc.

Figure 4.10. Display case, Texas Woman's University Library.
Photograph courtesy of Metropolitan Business Systems, Inc.

Figure 4.11. Rare book collection display cabinet, Western Theological Seminary Library. Photograph courtesy of Metropolitan Business Systems, Inc.

Figure 4.12. Stacks, library of a large law firm.

Figure 4.13. Open shelving.

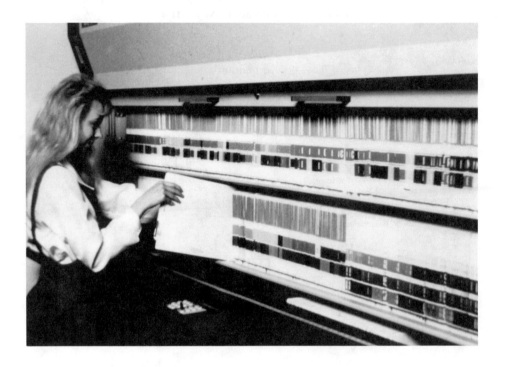

Figure 4.14. Remstar rotary file units. Photograph courtesy of
Metropolitan Business Systems, Inc.

PLANNING A MOBILE SHELVING SYSTEM

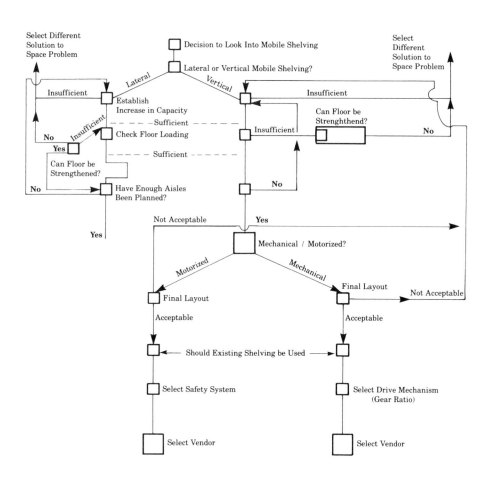

Figure 4.15. Planning a mobile shelving system. Reprinted with permission of Greenwood Press, Inc.

Figure 4.16. Lateral high density mobile shelving. Photograph courtesy of Supreme Equipment and Systems Corporation.

Figure 4.17. Spacesaver mechanical mobile shelving, Library for the Blind, Atlanta, GA. Photograph courtesy of Modern Office Systems.

Figure 4.18. Spacesaver mobile shelving, Winstead, McGuire, Sechrest & Minick. Photograph courtesy of Modern Office Systems.

Figure 4.19. Spacesaver electrical mobile shelving, Orange County Public Law Library. Photograph courtesy of Modern Office Systems.

access material in the back row, the shelving in front is moved to the left or right. There is no need for any electrical or mechanical help.

Vertical mobile shelving is used most often because it has the greatest storage capacity. Shelving sections are arranged so that the user faces the ends of the sections, which then move left or right to open a needed aisle. There are three types of vertical, high-density mobile shelving: manual, mechanical assist, and electrical. Manual and mechanical assist systems are used only for small shelving installations because a large shelving system would be too heavy to move manually. Electrical systems with safety mechanisms are installed for large shelving sections.

The system's size and volume of activity will determine the appropriate number of access points for the collection. Limited accessibility can be a drawback with high-density mobile shelving, especially with the vertical type. Access problems result when insufficient aisles are provided and workers have to wait until an aisle is available. To avoid this problem, consider activity rates. Know the daily activity level in, and the number of staff requiring simultaneous access to, a shelving section.

Waegemann's equation (1985) may be used to compute the required number of aisles. The number of people requiring simultaneous access during peak hours multiplied by the increase in storage capacity over the conventional storage equipment currently being used equals the number of aisles to be planned for the mobile shelving system. For example, if an existing system has four people retrieving collection materials from a shelving section during peak hours, and the planned mobile shelving system will have a 70% increase in storage capacity over the existing system (this means a 1.7 increase in capacity because the existing system has a factor of 1.0), the number of aisles required is seven. (See Figure 4.20.)

Figure 4.20. Formula for Computing the Number of Aisles in a Mobile Shelving System[+]

$$4 \text{ (people)} \times 1.7 \text{ (increase factor)} = 6.8$$

[+]"High Density Storage Equipment," *The Records and Retrieval Report,* C. Peter Waegemann, ed. May 1985, Vol. 1, No. 5., pp. 81-82.

Floor load capacity is the most important planning factor when you are considering high-density mobile shelving. It is important to determine the weight of the installation and whether the floor can support the load. Since high-density mobile shelving can store nearly double the volume of material in a conventional storage system, the floor must be able to hold twice the load. To avoid problems, compute the weight of the system fully loaded.

To do this, request from the vendor the total weight of the high-density mobile storage system when empty. Then, determine the "payload" weight of the material to be housed on the high-density mobile storage equipment. The payload is computed by weighing material on a few typical shelving sections, then dividing this weight by the number of linear inches occupied on a shelf and multiplying the weight by the proposed shelving capacity. This will equal the number of payload pounds. Adding the payload to the weight of the high-density mobile storage system will give the total weight. Finally, structural engineers should compare the payload to the live and distributed load factors of the area to see if the floor can support the weight. If not, the floor may be strengthened structurally.

Terry Day, a systems consultant for Supreme Equipment and Systems Corporation in Brooklyn, New York, has a formula to determine how much weight can be put in an area:

1. Gather five books that measure a total of six inches (include a sampling of all widths of books).

2. Weigh each book and divide by the number of inches of the width of the book to obtain the weight per linear inch. For example, the first book may weigh six pounds and measure three inches, which when divided by six equals two pounds per inch. The next book may weigh twelve pounds and measure three inches; twelve divided by three equals four pounds per inch.

3. Add the total weight of the sample inches and divide by five (for the five books) for an average of the pounds per inch.

4. Measure the total linear inches of books.

5. Multiply the inches of books by the average pounds per inch. This will be the weight of the books.

6. Divide the weight into the number of square feet of floor space to get the pounds per square foot that the books will be exerting on the floor.

For example, 5,000 inches of books at two pounds per inch equals 10,000 pounds of books. If the high-density mobile storage weighs 20,000 pounds, 30,000 pounds is exerted on the floor. If these books are to be stored in an area ten feet by ten feet, or 100 square feet, divide the square feet into the number of pounds, which yields 300 pounds per square foot. The weight per square foot would be reduced if the same amount of books was stored over a larger area. Five hundred square feet of space holding the same weight would mean sixty pounds per square foot. Widening aisles between high-density mobile shelving also disperses and reduces the floor load. Floor-load capacity is discussed in greater detail in Chapter 2, "Evaluating the Building."

Shelves can store a variety of materials, e.g., documents, records, microforms, indexes, art books, musical scores, and audio- and video-cassettes. Thus, if space is available and the floor can support or be reinforced to support the installation, vertical mobile shelving is recommended for most libraries.

Newspapers and periodicals are usually placed on library shelves, although some libraries separate unbound current issues from bound older issues of periodicals and place them in different locations. Current issues are placed on newspaper sticks hung on racks or in stack inserts.

Cabinets

Several types of file cabinets are effective in libraries. Vertical and lateral file cabinets are used for filing papers and pamphlets, and lateral, or flat files, are used for maps and engineering and architectural drawings. Flat files usually come in five-drawer units which stack on top of each other. Lateral files are generally easier to use than vertical files and provide greater storage capacity. They require less aisle space than standard vertical file cabinets.

Standard vertical file cabinet drawers extend twenty-eight inches into an aisle and require at least five feet of aisle space for traffic; 7 ½ to 8 feet of aisle space if two rows of vertical file cabinets face each other. Standard lateral file cabinet drawers extend eighteen inches into an aisle and require 4 ½ feet for traffic—six feet of aisle space if two rows of lateral file cabinets face each other.

Lateral files are available in several widths, thirty-six inches being the most common. Both vertical and lateral cabinets are available in legal and letter size and in many different heights.

Storage cabinets may be needed for audiovisual equipment, telephone books, atlases, microforms, and office supplies. As discussed in Chapter 6, "Library Technology," computer-based resources and micrographic technology require adequate storage space for computer paper, disks (including floppy and optical disks, especially CD-ROM), microfilm rolls and cartridges, microfiche sheets and aperture cards, software and hardware documentation, bulbs, cleaners, and spare parts.

Card Catalogs

While it is recommended that a special library convert its card catalog to an automated system (see Chapter 6, "Library Technology"), some libraries may still be using a hard copy card catalog system. Most card catalogs are constructed of wood, which is more durable and less noisy than metal cabinets when drawers are opened. Cabinets are usually sixty- or seventy-two-drawer units and can be purchased in fifteen, seventeen, and nineteen-inch lengths. The seventeen-inch size is recommended because it is easy to use and has a large capacity. Placing a reference table nearby is helpful for browsing through the catalog.

Other Equipment

A fully functioning special library will require other equipment. Do not overlook these items when designing the library; they consume space and electricity and may generate noise. These items include step stools, ladders, book trucks, pamphlet displays, dictionary stands, photocopiers, typewriters, calculators, and clocks.

Figure 4.21. Flat files, Texas A&M University Library, College Station, TX. Photograph courtesy of Metropolitan Business Systems, Inc.

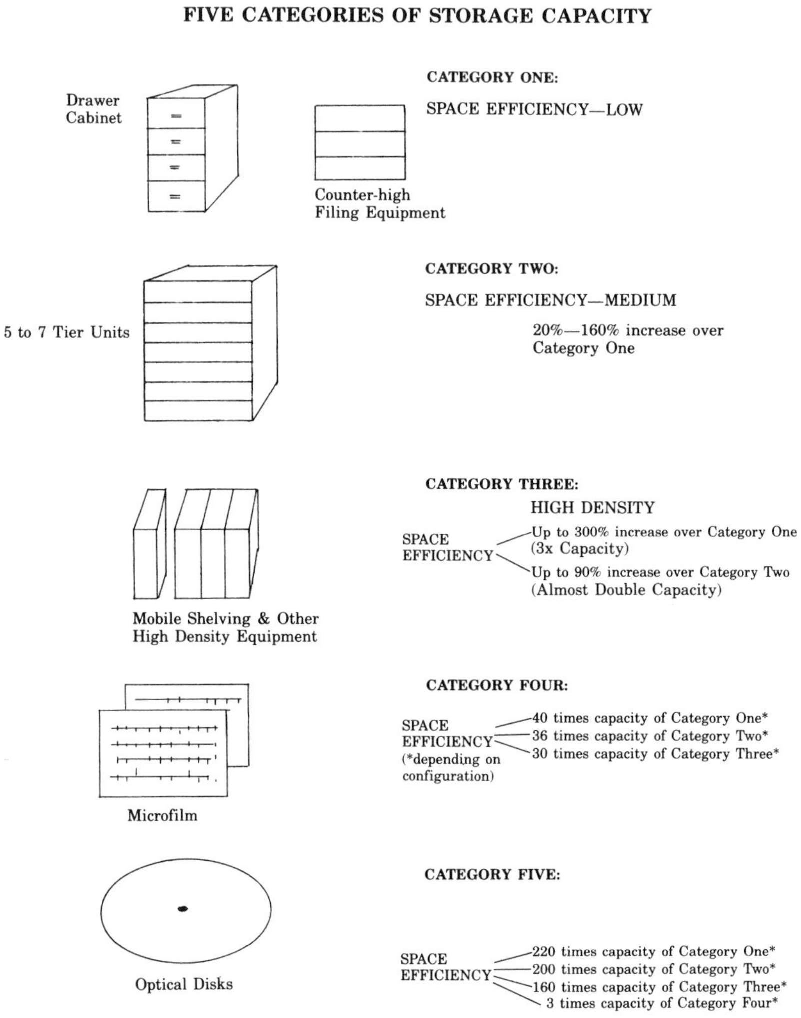

FIVE CATEGORIES OF STORAGE CAPACITY

Drawer
Cabinet

CATEGORY ONE:

SPACE EFFICIENCY—LOW

Counter-high
Filing Equipment

5 to 7 Tier Units

CATEGORY TWO:

SPACE EFFICIENCY—MEDIUM

20%—160% increase over
Category One

CATEGORY THREE:

HIGH DENSITY

SPACE
EFFICIENCY

Up to 300% increase over Category One
(3x Capacity)

Up to 90% increase over Category Two
(Almost Double Capacity)

Mobile Shelving & Other
High Density Equipment

CATEGORY FOUR:

SPACE
EFFICIENCY
(*depending on
configuration)

40 times capacity of Category One*
36 times capacity of Category Two*
30 times capacity of Category Three*

Microfilm

CATEGORY FIVE:

SPACE
EFFICIENCY

220 times capacity of Category One*
200 times capacity of Category Two*
160 times capacity of Category Three*
3 times capacity of Category Four*

Optical Disks

Figure 4.22. Five categories of storage capacity. Reprinted with permission of Greenwood Press, Inc.

**GUIDE TO INCREASES IN FILING CAPACITY USING
ALTERNATE STORAGE EQUIPMENT IN PLACE OF
FOUR-DRAWER LETTER-SIZE CABINETS**

Five-drawer cabinet	20%
Letter-sized lateral file, open shelving type	
5-tier	60%
6-tier	89%
7-tier	118%
8-tier	146%
Letter-sized lateral file, enclosed with doors, 6-tier	43%
Times-two cabinet	
5-tier, stand-alone	49%
5-tier, as add-on unit	71%
6-tier, stand-alone	75%
6-tier, as add-on unit	102%
7-tier, stand-alone	101%
7-tier, as add-on unit	133%
8-tier, stand-alone	128%
8-tier, as add-on unit	164%
Power files	
14 carriers	79%
16 carriers	102%
18 carriers	125%
Lateral mobile shelving, 2-tier	
6 shelves	158%
7 shelves	198%
8 shelves	238%
Lateral mobile shelving, 3-tier	
6 shelves	218%
7 shelves	268%
8 shelves	318%
Vertical mobile shelving, 6-foot sections, 4 sections per aisle	
6 shelves	202%
7 shelves	256%
8 shelves	305%
Vertical mobile shelving, 9-foot sections, 4 sections per aisle	
6 shelves	239%
7 shelves	294%
8 shelves	336%

Figure 4.23. Guide to increases in filing capacity. Reprinted with permission from Greenwood Press, Inc.

Space Efficiency Factors

	File Placed Singularly			File Sharing an Aisle		
	Sq. Ft.	LFFs	Space Efficiency Factor	Sq. Ft.	LFFs	Space Efficiency Factor
Low efficiency						
2-drawer, legal-size cabinet	11.75	4	2.93	9.37	4	2.34
2-drawer, letter-size cabinet	9.75	4	2.43	7.87	4	1.96
3-drawer, legal-size cabinet	11.75	6	1.95	9.37	6	1.56
3-drawer, letter-size cabinet	9.75	6	1.62	7.87	6	1.31
4-drawer insulated security cabinet	12.75	8	1.62	10.37	8	1.29
4-drawer, legal-size cabinet	11.75	8	1.46	9.37	8	1.17
4-drawer, letter-size cabinet	9.75	8	1.21	7.87	8	.98
5-drawer, legal-size cabinet	11.75	10	1.18	9.37	10	.94
3-tier, counter-high, lateral file	10.50	9	1.17	6.75	9	.75
Intermediate efficiency						
5-drawer, letter-size cabinet	9.75	10	.98	7.87	10	.79
5-tier, X-ray open shelf or legal file with doors	12.00	15	.80	8.25	15	.55
Minitrieve (Supreme), letter-size, with work station M/T 0903	143.00	202	.71			
5-tier, circular rotary file Giro-oblique	14.00	20	.70			
(If inner space is taken into account [50%])	14.00	30	.46			
6-tier, legal-size lateral file	12.00	18	.66	8.25	18	.45
6-tier, letter-size file	10.50	18	.58	6.75	18	.37
7-tier, lateral file with Databoxes	10.50	19	.55	6.75	19	.35
7-tier, letter-size file	10.50	21	.50	6.75	21	.32
8-tier, open-shelf, letter-size, lateral file	10.50	24	.43	6.75	24	.28
High-density storage-high space efficiency						
Times Two or Rotomatic, letter-size						
5-shelf high, stand-alone	15.90	20.8	.76	11.96	20.8	.57
5-shelf, as add-on unit	13.56	20.8	.65	10.18	20.8	.49
6-shelf, stand-alone	15.90	25	.64	10.18	25	.48
6-shelf, as add-on unit	13.56	25	.54	10.18	25	.41
7-shelf, stand-alone	15.90	29.2	.55	11.96	29.2	.41
7-shelf, as add-on unit	13.56	29.2	.46	10.18	29.2	.35
8-shelf, stand-alone	15.9	33.3	.48	11.96	33.3	.36
8-shelf, as add-on unit	13.56	33.3	.41	10.18	33.3	.31
Power files						
14 carriers	63.75	102.83	.62	53.2	102.8	.52
16 carriers	63.75	117.5	.54	53.2	117.5	.45
18 carriers	63.75	132.2	.48	53.2	132.2	.40
Minitrieve, letter-size, including work station						
M/T 0909	284.00	607	.47			
M/T 0915	363.00	1015	.36			
M/T 0920	451.00	1350	.33			
M/T 0925	439.00	1687	.26			
Lateral letter-size, mobile shelving, Bifile or similar						
6-shelf, 2 tiers	15.00	36	.41	11.25	36	31
7-shelf, 2-tiers	15.00	42	.35	11.25	42	.26
8-shelf, 2-tiers	15.00	48	.31	11.25	48	.23

(Cont.)

Figure 4.24. Space efficiency factors. Reprinted with permission from Greenwood Press, Inc.

	File Placed Singularly			File Sharing an Aisle		
	Sq. Ft.	*LFFs*	*Space Efficiency Factor*	*Sq. Ft.*	*LFFs*	*Space Efficiency Factor*
Trifile or similar						
6-shelf, 3-tiers	18.00	54	.33	15.75	54	.29
7-shelf, 3-tiers	18.00	63	.28	15.75	63	.25
8-shelf, 3-tiers	18.00	72	.25	15.75	72	.21
9 feet deep	100.62	324	.31	89.68	324	.27
12 feet deep	126.87	432	.29	115.93	432	.26
Vertical mobile shelving, letter-size, 7 shelves						
3 feet deep	48.12	126	.38	37.18	126	.29
6 feet deep	74.37	252	.29	63.45	252	.25
9 feet deep	100.62	378	.26	89.68	378	.24
12 feet deep	126.87	504	.25	115.93	504	.23
Vertical mobile shelving, letter-size, 8 shelves						
3 feet deep	48.12	144	.33	37.18	144	.26
6 feet deep	74.37	288	.26	63.45	288	.22
9 feet deep	100.62	432	.23	89.68	432	.21
12 feet deep	126.87	576	.22	115.9	576	.20
Vertical mobile shelving, X-ray-size or oversized, 18 inches deep, 5 shelves high, 3 double sections per aisle						
3 feet deep	64.63	90	.72	49.94	90	.55
6 feet deep	97.75	180	.54	83.37	180	.46
9 feet deep	132.25	270	.48	117.87	270	.43
12 feet deep	166.75	360	.46	152.37	360	.42
Vertical mobile shelving, letter-size, 6 shelves						
3 feet deep	48.12	108	.44	37.18	108	.34
6 feet deep	74.37	216	.34	63.45	216	.29

Figure 4.25. Card catalog, Western Theological Seminary Library.
Photograph courtesy of Metropolitan Business Systems, Inc.

The kind and amount of furniture and equipment in the special library will be influenced by collection requirements, space constraints, and user needs. Equally important to the overall effectiveness of the library is ergonomics, the relationship between the furniture and equipment and the people who use it.

Chapter 5. Ergonomics and Space Planning

ERGONOMICS HAS COME OF AGE because office planners and designers realize that well-designed offices will result from considering all factors in the planning stages. Ergonomics is the relationship of humans to their work environment. It involves reconciling the essential factors in an office to produce comfortable and productive work environments. Some concepts associated with ergonomics include:

1. systems analysis;

2. job analysis;

3. time and work studies;

4. the proper tools and hardware for the worker;

5. human physiology;

6. behavioral responses of workers to their work environments; and

7.   external factors that affect workers both physically and
     psychologically, e.g., light, temperature, sound, color,
     texture, shape, decor, and appearance.

Ergonomics also deals with how people interact with machines. Such equipment factors as keyboard arrangement, printer location, and type of computer screen affect productivity and worker satisfaction.

Anthropometrics

Anthropometrics is the study of human shapes and sizes, or the study of human body measurements for the correct scaling of sizes, heights, and shapes of furniture and equipment.

Chairs

The height of a desk and chair is important for working comfort. Poorly designed seating greatly contributes to office fatigue. Using seats designed for correct posture not only decreases fatigue, but it also increases efficiency. Adjustable chairs and desks facilitate correct posture and accommodate different sizes of people. Such chairs are necessary for all office work.

The mean base of a chair is between seventeen and eighteen inches from the floor so that the user's feet are flat on the floor. Select chairs allowing four adjustments: seat height, back height, back depth, and back spring tension. Use a chair with casters for mobility and five legs for stability. Purchase a chair with material that allows for ventilation and sound absorption, as well as durability. Use a seat cushion that slopes in the front to improve circulation and eliminate pressure on the underside of legs above the knees.

Desks

Desk height also affects work efficiency. Although most desks are twenty-seven inches from the floor, desks can be adjusted in height. Although twenty-eight inches is appropriate for approximately 80 percent of the people, the adjustment should range from twenty-seven to thirty inches. The desk top needs to be approximately twenty-seven inches if a typewriter or other machine is to be used on it. Typewriter platforms should be four inches lower than a regular desk top. Desks also should be durable and have a nonreflective surface so that light will not shine into readers' eyes.

Tables and Carrels

Like desks, tables should not have highly polished surfaces that reflect light. Table tops should be twenty to thirty inches from the floor. Individual tables and carrels are preferable to larger tables intended for several workers. The working surface should be at least four feet wide and two feet deep to enable users to have several books and a pad of paper. Carrels should also have a raised storage shelf which permits material not in use to be placed above the working surface. Many users prefer a row of small, partially enclosed alcoves against a long wall rather than ready-made carrels.

Computer Workstations/VDT Screens/Monitors

The National Institute of Occupational Safety and Health found that computer operators most often complained of glare, poor illumination, and poorly designed workstations. For this reason, ergonomics plays a key role in the development of computer workstations and accessories.

Eyestrain, musculoskeletal strain, and morale problems are associated repeatedly with VDT screens. Prevention involves two basic factors: all components of the workstation must be designed to accommodate the specific tasks and equipment requirements, and all components of the workstation must be engineered to support the physical and psychological needs of the user. The design of the workstation should permit flexibility in size, shape, height, configuration, ease of use, and adaptability.

When designing the workstation, make sure that:

1. The worker's eyes are horizontal with the top of the display screen;

2. The viewing angle is 30 to 40 degrees;

3. The distance from the worker's eyes to the screen is thirteen to twenty-four inches;

4. The center of the screen is ten to sixteen inches above the keyboard support surface;

5. The screen tilts or swivels to help adjust for glare and to ease muscle strain in the neck and shoulders;

6. The source documents are as close to the screen as possible to reduce eye movement and eye strain;

7. The viewing distance between the worker and the source document is kept approximately the same as the distance between the worker and the screen to make it easier for the worker's eyes to focus; and

8. The screen is placed parallel to windows and ceiling lights to reduce glare; if not, a glass or plastic glare filter or screen should be used.

Biomechanics

Biomechanics is the study of the musculoskeletal effort of human beings. Biomechanical factors help in the design of work spaces and layouts that minimize work strain, thus increasing productivity and decreasing errors. The placement of supplies or a telephone at a workstation is extremely important. If these items are not located conveniently and reached easily, the worker is forced to bend and stretch, often placing great strain on the musculoskeletal system.

Hands and wrists that can not lean or rest on the keyboard contribute to muscular strain. Placing wrist rests next to a keyboard provides needed support and reduces muscular stress and fatigue. Swivel tilt bases enable computer terminal adjustment to provide glare-free, comfortable viewing.

Psychological Considerations

Psychological considerations are factors, such as sound, temperature, ventilation, color, and light, that can affect workers physically and psychologically.

Figure 5.1. Biotic Systems computer work station. Photograph courtesy of Metropolitan Business Systems, Inc.

Noise

Noise attacks the nervous system and creates lethargy, nervous strain, and fatigue. It can result in absenteeism, affect a worker's ability to make decisions, and cause physical and medical problems. Although people adapt to noise, they never become totally accustomed to it. Long exposure to noises of more than seventy decibels can permanently impair hearing. The noise level at the average office is approximately fifty decibels. A noisy office is between sixty and eighty decibels, roughly equal to a factory. In a word/data processing department that has no acoustical treatment, the level could climb to 100 decibels.

Proper ergonomic planning can decrease noise levels. Acoustically treated ceilings, floors, and walls reduce office noise levels; drapes insulate and protect against excessive light and noise; and carpeting improves the acoustic quality of floors. In addition, typewriters and other office machines should not be placed in front of steel partitions or on desks that will reflect sound.

Temperature, Humidity, and Ventilation

Poor ventilation can reduce a worker's efficiency 10 to 20 percent. When the air is stale and too warm, employees feel drowsy and tired. Good ventilation introduces fresh air, dispels used air, moves air without drafts, maintains 50 percent humidity, and cleans the air. Air-conditioning systems and modern filters do this. One study showed that work output for those in air-conditioned offices increased by more than 9 percent over those in offices without air-conditioning (Place and Popham, 1966).

Offices that are too cold also inhibit work. In one situation, an office was air-conditioned to such a point—30 degrees F, far colder than it would be in winter with heating—that staff had to wear heavy sweaters, gloves, and earmuffs. This affected productivity, energy level, and emotional and physical well being. Staff members became sick often during the project, particularly because the outside temperatures of 80-90 degrees F were a drastic contrast.

Too much dampness causes mold and mildew, which affect respiration and health. In one case, the nursing school of a large eastern hospital needed its archival nursing collection reorganized and preserved. The school had been vacant since the 1960s and one room had been shut since the 1930s. The project began in the winter, and the environment was damp with mold and mildew. Workers suffered from respiratory infections, sinus headaches, allergies and other health problems. Many quit the project because of the hazardous working conditions.

People can adapt to temperature levels by wearing heavier clothing, but temperature, humidity, and air distribution also affect equipment performance. If relative humidity falls below 25 percent, static can build up and affect some equipment. Likewise, computer equipment is affected by high temperature and humidity. One eastern university set up its computer laboratory with a temperature of 85-90 degrees F and humidity of approximately 85 percent. As a result, computer equipment broke down and the university needed frequent service calls to repair the equipment which could have been avoided if the university had considered ergonomics and the correct temperature and humidity for such sensitive equipment.

Color

Color in an office is not simply a matter of decoration or good taste. It also affects the diffusion of light. Light greens, light blues, buffs, and greys are used for office walls, and whites for ceilings. Bright touches of color relieve monotony and give warmth and interest to a room. In one instance of poor color choice, a large eastern law firm redecorated its library. The firm's interior designer chose various shades of grey. Although terrific for a penthouse apartment or even a reception area, the color selection was fatal for staff and users. The pure tonality of the library caused inefficiency, drowsiness, lethargy, and lack of productivity.

Colors have different absorption rates according to the amount of white or black they contain. (See Figure 5.2.)

Figure 5.2. Color Values

Color	Reflection (%)
White	80–90
Light Green	55–65
Light Blue	45–55
Brown	5–15
Buff	60–70

furnishing and equipment. Colors, textures, and patterns of ceilings, wall, floors, draperies, and other furnishings should blend together. One can change the perceived size and shape of an area with color; light colors, for example, appear to advance and dark ones appear to recede.

Figure 5.2. Color Values

Color	Reflection (%)
White	80–90
Light Green	55–65
Light Blue	45–55
Brown	5–15
Buff	60–70
Light Grey	50–60
Dark Green	7–20

In another example of color used improperly, a new chief operating officer of a financial public relations firm bought purple and brown paint because it was on sale. Workers returning to the office after a long weekend found themselves inside offices that caused migraine headaches, nausea, unrest, and agitation, to name just a few of the complaints. The cost to repaint the office (including many coats of white paint) far exceeded the cost of painting the office correctly the first time. In addition, office productivity and morale were at an all-time low because of the first painting fiasco. Another organization specified dark walls to reduce glare. Instead, however, the dark walls produced tension in office workers, re-duced productivity and energy levels, inhibited workers from communicating with each other and with workers in lighter-walled areas, and made the workers more irritable.

Color can change and enliven the clinical environment that may result when lighting in a library has been designed primarily for seeing efficiently.

Energy

Businesses today are concerned with energy and energy conservation. Companies are reducing consumption for heating, lighting, and air-conditioning. Many newer buildings use the heat generated by lighting and recirculate it as part of the total heating system. Similar conservation attempts are being considered for electricity.

Lighting

Efficient and effective office illumination has been a major corporate goal for years. Better illumination is directly related to increases in effort and office productivity. Light bounced off shiny surfaces produces glare, which causes eyestrain, headaches, and decreased productivity, and is the greatest cause of fatigue in the office today. In addition to causing visual problems, poor lighting can adversely affect employee morale. Finally, lighting consumes more energy than all office components.

Natural light is not always available, so both natural and artificial light are used. Whenever possible, rows of book stacks or file cabinets should be at right angles to windows to allow light to penetrate the aisles and fall across the contents of book shelves and file drawers.

Lighting affects space allocation, especially in open shelving areas where it should be placed between shelving units that face each other in aisles. Lighting is also crucial for computer and other office work.

Glare

Both direct and indirect glare can cause great problems. Indirect glare results when light shines on a surface and then reflects into a person's eyes. Many lighting systems create a form of indirect glare called "veiling reflections," which occur when the light source is directly in front of, and above, a person's line of sight. Light bounces from a work surface into a person's eyes and reduces contrast between background and the work surface. Moving the work surface or the lighting fixture can eliminate this problem.

Direct glare occurs when light shines directly into someone's line of sight. In offices, improperly shielded fixtures can cause direct glare when lamps are level with the line of sight. Direct glare also can be caused by sunlight through a window.

Light Spill

Light spill is the configuration of light once it leaves the bulb or fixture. Every light bulb, fixture, panel, or mirror surface produces a different type of spill, so it is very important to carefully choose the lighting for a library. In addition, changing anything about the lighting system (e.g., the angle at which a beam is discharged) might change the spill. Aside from variations in the light spill from bulb to bulb, fixture design also creates variation. Therefore, light spill should always be considered.

Shadows

Shadows are another lighting concern. They can be a source of discomfort or distraction when they are in a person's line of sight. A downward-directed light that is not diffused can cause shadows. In reading/reviewing areas, staff areas, and book stacks, the lighting should be scattered (i.e., as evenly diffused as possible) to avoid shadowing problems.

Stack Lighting

Stacks can be lighted in one of five ways:

1. *Fluorescent or High-Intensity Discharge (HID) fixtures attached to the ceiling in a grid pattern.* This requires a minimum three-foot clearance between the tops of shelving and the ceiling and is the most flexible lighting system. With this lighting, the planner can place stacks in any direction, and the lighting fixtures will be close enough to light them. This configuration is excellent for high ceilings, when HID or special types of fluorescent fixtures, e.g., bat-wing fixtures, are used. However, it wastes energy in low ceilings where lighting must be placed irrespective of the location of the stacks.

2. *Fixtures affixed to the ceiling, parallel to the stacks, and running down the center of the aisles.* No clearance above the stack is needed unless there is a ceiling sprinkler installation. This is the recommended configuration for fixed/ stationary stacks. The entire front of each stack can be lighted with this arrangement. However, avoid light spills

that can cast shadows if the lighting is not installed correctly. If the size of the stack area changes causing stacks to be moved, the lighting will also have to be moved. This configuration conserves energy because lights are near the stacks they illuminate and no light is lost over the top of the stack.

3. *Fixtures ceiling mounted parallel to the stacks, running directly above each stack.* These lights need at least one foot of clearance above the stack. In this case, the lighting fixture should be mounted directly over the top of the stack, using a bat-wing fixture. However, this configuration is often difficult to install correctly. In addition, because the light tends to shine sideways, it can be reflected off the bookbindings, creating a strange color.

4. *Fixtures ceiling mounted perpendicular to the stacks.* At least one foot of clearance is needed above the stacks. Lighting should be placed four feet-six inches to six feet on center. Some light is lost over the tops of the stacks, but the angle of the light, because of the perpendicular configuration, covers all the shelves. Stacks can be moved without calculating exactly how the light will fall. This system is good for ceilings nine feet and lower and is the correct configuration for high-density vertical mobile shelving where the arrangement of stacks varies according to which aisle is opened.

5. *Integrated Lighting Systems.* In these systems, lighting fixtures are a part of the book stacks (i.e., the stacks come with lights installed along with tops) and light bulbs rest directly on the stacks. The ceiling becomes a secondary light source because the stack-affixed lighting illuminates the ceiling and reflects on the stacks. A three-foot clearance from the ceiling and stack-affixed lighting is required to ensure correct illumination of the ceiling.

Lighting Fixtures

Lighting fixtures, or luminaries, can be grouped into four types: incandescent, fluorescent, high-intensity discharge (HID), and low-pressure discharge.

1. *Incandescent.* These bulbs are expensive in terms of energy consumption. They consume approximately 90 percent of their electrical energy as heat, which can interfere with a library's heating, ventilating and air-conditioning system.

2. *Fluorescent.* These bulbs are the most commonly used lighting in libraries today. They afford a minimum of three times the light per unit of energy and two to sixteen times the life of a comparable incandescent bulb. Fluorescents are also more diffuse and less bright than incandescents. Fluorescent light transmits a glow instead of a beam and produces a cool light, much cooler than the light produced by an incandescent. All lighting gives off heat, which in the summer becomes part of the air-conditioning load, so it is best to select the lighting that generates the least heat.

3. *High-Intensity Discharge (HID).* These bulbs are similar to fluorescent in how they produce light. A HID bulb is protected by an outer glass cover that resists heat, minimizes drafts, and absorbs electromagnetic rays. These bulbs conserve energy and have a long life. HID bulbs might shut off during major electrical current variations and might have to cool off before they light up again. They must warm up before they reach full output.

4. *Low-Pressure Discharge.* These bulbs are similar to HIDs and conserve the most energy. They cast a yellow-brown light rather than white light, but once this peculiarity has been corrected, their use in libraries undoubtedly will be more widespread.

Figure 5.3. The "Arc Reach." Photograph courtesy of Paul Leung.

In addition to these stack lighting and light bulb options, libraries can use task-ambient lighting, which is lighting set into individual workstations, carrels, and book stacks.

If circumstances allow, it is always best to purchase fixtures that vent. As the heat tends to rise, a small draft will carry away the dirt that forms in and around the bulb and housing. In other words, the bulbs will be cleaner and function more efficiently.

The standard for normal office work is fifty foot candles. A foot candle is a unit of light measure that approximates the light of a candle one foot from its flame. Lighting throughout a library should be at least twenty-five foot candles at about desk height.

Principles of Motion Economy

Saving energy and eliminating unnecessary motions influence how items are arranged on a desk. When planning a library, take into consideration these principles of motion economy: the arc reach, rules of minimum effort, distribution of effort, space and tool use, and general energy savers.

Arc Reach

Think about the way an arm swings from the shoulder. It swings in an arc. Because arced desks are not easy to manufacture, workers compromise and butt together two rectangular desks, a desk and table, or a desk and file cabinet. This produces a functional work area that complements the swing of the arm. (see Figure 5-3.)

Part of the arc reach principle takes into account how far one can reach comfortably. The well-designed and well-organized workstation has regularly used materials located within the arc of easy reach. A functional desk should be only thirty inches deep. Although deeper ones are available, these are used primarily for executive prestige.

Rules of Minimum Effort

Someone who is working energetically is not necessarily working efficiently. The following suggestions, from *Filing and Records Management* by Irene Place and Estelle Popham (Englewood Cliffs, NJ: Prentice-Hall, 1966, p. 220) can be applied to library activities:

1. Have work come to the worker to cut down on interruptions, e.g., use "in" baskets.

2. Release the hands from unnecessary work whenever possible, e.g., shoulder telephone holder, telephone speaker phone, mail chute.

3. Mechanize, e.g., use electric pencil sharpeners, staplers, and hole punchers.

4. Batch work, thus cutting down on make-ready and put-away activities, e.g., sort material before processing or filing.

5. Eliminate the nonessential, e.g., use continuous pin-feed computer labels.

Distribution of Effort

When both hands are working, complementary motions should be used. Avoid using one hand as a holder while the other works. Perform a work pattern so that it is smooth, rhythmic, and continuous. Confine body movements so energy is not wasted. For example, when hands will do a job, do not strain arms or shoulders (Place and Popham, 1966).

Space and Tool Use

Locate materials so the best sequence of motions can be used in reaching and using them. Pre-position materials used regularly, have a definite place for each article, and give priority to the location of frequently used items (Place and Popham 1966).

Work Flow

When considering work flow, remember that a straight line is still the shortest distance between two points. Desks, tables, and books should be arranged so that work flows in a straight line from receiving to processing, and finally to book and record filing operations. There should be a minimum amount of backtracking. Work should flow directly from one desk to another and then to the stacks.

As mentioned previously, the coordination of a library with the units or departments it serves may depend on the flow of material. It is desirable to have material flow efficiently to and from, and within, a library.

The most productive workers will be those who are most comfortable in their working environment. The library space planner must account for all the ergonomic factors discussed in this chapter to achieve this goal.

Chapter 6. Library Technology

AS INFORMATION TECHNOLOGY advances, is refined, and expands its applications, the special library depends increasingly on technologically based resources and services. Resources will always be available in paper, but librarians will more often choose electronic and magnetic-based resources because of their convenience, durability, and integrity. The new electronic special library must be planned differently from its predecessors to accommodate state-of-the-art information services.

Electronic and magnetic-based library resources require different kinds and amounts of space than their paper counterparts. Information can be stored more compactly on these media than on paper. Magnetic and optical media are more durable. Unfortunately, the initial costs for creating the magnetic- or optical-based library are high, but ultimately, savings are realized in space, the time spent sorting and replacing damaged materials, and the time used processing paper-based subscriptions to journals, indexes and abstracts, periodicals, and other bulk information.

Space considerations for the technologically advanced special library should include the location of the computer hardware, namely, terminals, modems, printers, plotters, and many other peripherals; and storage space for the supplies, manuals, directories, backup disks and tapes, and telecommunications equipment.

Optical disk technology is an important information technology of special libraries. This technology comes in the form of erasable disks, compact disk-read only memory (CD-ROM), video disks, and nonerasable write once/read many (WORM) disks. Other technologies discussed in this Chapter include satellite transmission systems, on-line services, microform, computer output microfilm (COM), and in-house data bases. Other significant technologies such as telefacsimile, electronic mail, and local area networks are discussed in Chapter 7, "Increasing Resource Sharing."

Optical Disk Technology

Optical disks store data electronically, and the storage capacity is much greater than magnetic disks. Depending on the size of the optical disk and the compression ratio, one optical may equal 1200 floppy disks. The optical technologies with the greatest impact on special libraries and information centers are erasable and nonerasable optical disks. This includes CD-ROM, WORM, and video disks.

Erasable Optical Disks

There are several types of erasable optical disks, but presently, the magneto-optical disk is the format of choice. The other types of erasable disks are phase change technology and dye-based. The magneto-optical drive's capacity greatly surpasses that of a conventional hard disk.[1] Approximately one billion bytes (1 gigabyte) of data can be stored on the magneto-optical disk.

Until recently, optical disks were not erasable because changes made on the surface of a recording layer could not be reversed. Because some information management applications require the ability to change and update information on an ongoing basis, the optical disks' nonerasable feature was a major drawback.

Erasable disks are the newest and most promising area of optical storage. Erasable drives let you write, erase, and read data just as hard disks do. Erasable disks finally became available late in 1988.

The standard hard disk in a personal computer stores 20-200 megabytes of data.[2] Like the floppy disk, optical disks are removable from the personal computer. Substantial amounts of research material can be placed on the optical disk and used on different computers.

Nonerasable Optical Disks
Compact Disk-Read Only Memory (CD-ROM)
CD-ROM distributes large amounts of digital information, either on a stand-alone system or as part of the local area network (LAN). A special license and additional fees are required from the publisher if the CD-ROM is used on a network. The CD-ROM disk can hold more than 540 megabytes of data or the equivalent of 200,000 printed pages.[3]

Unlike information stored on the floppy disk, CD-ROM data cannot be altered (hence the term, "write once/read only"). However, information from the CD-ROM can be downloaded from the disk to another program file (e.g., word processing or a spreadsheet) and edited with the appropriate software interface. Any information that can be converted to digital form, such as text, graphics, or audio-visual material, can be stored on CD-ROM.[4]

The federal government publishes such data as the consumer price index, interest rate topics, and agricultural, food and labor statistics on CD-ROM. The *Electronic Encyclopedia,* published by Grolier, is available on CD-ROM, as is *Webster's Ninth Collegiate Dictionary.*[5]

Because of the high costs associated with the manufacture of the master CD-ROM disk, only widely distributed information should be considered for a CD-ROM application. An organization that creates in-house data bases can use CD-ROM to store and distribute that information. A service bureau can assist with the preparation of the data bases for recording and can oversee the production of the disks.

Write Once Read Many (WORM)
A WORM optical storage device (also referred to as Direct Read After Write , or DRAW) permits the storage of information once; it cannot be erased or changed. Because the data cannot be altered, WORM is used mostly for archival storage to protect the

integrity of data. WORM can be used to make backup copies of hard disk storage. Blank disks are purchased and information is recorded on the disks from the keyboard, scanner, magnetic media, or other sources.

Some companies distribute manuals, corporate annual reports, and other data on WORM so that new data or material can be added to the existing disk.[6] Widespread acceptance of WORM has been hindered by its expense. However, costs for larger applications are decreasing and new, less expensive microcomputer-based systems have encouraged more companies to consider this technology.

Space Planning Considerations for Optical Storage

Most of the optical technology applications in special libraries will be microcomputer based. CD-ROM applications run on a personal computer that has a CD-ROM drive attached. Other optical storage disks (e.g., WORM and erasable) also run on a personal computer equipped with the appropriate disk drive. Some repro- gramming of the DOS program files will be required to accommo- date the optical disk drives.

Analog video disks run on video disk players that can be accommodated by a four-foot wide surface. A digital video disk player is used as a peripheral to the personal computer or multi- user system, and requires a thirty-inch surface.[7] Adequate electric power should be available.

Space should be allocated for the hardware, as well as for disk collections, manuals, computer paper, and ribbons. When planning the storage space, growth and expansion should be considered because disk-based resources will accumulate over time.

Satellite Information Systems

Recent developments in the satellite industry have made it more advantageous for organizations to use satellite-based systems for the transfer of information. Satellites can link branch offices of an organization so that critical information can be delivered quickly. Several recent developments in the industry make it more economi- cal and practical for an organization to establish satellite communi- cation links. Among these developments are transponder space (the satellite transmitter) and the availability of smaller and less expensive hardware.[8] Private systems, VSATs (very small aperture terminals), or the satellite dish are highly economical systems.

For a large and geographically diverse organization that uses satellite communication, the planners of the special library should consider linking the library or information center to the satellite system. Satellites can be used for document delivery, as well as text, voice, or image-based data.[9]

Electronic document delivery via satellite has several advantages:

1. Large amounts of information are distributed at fast speeds; there is a low error rate; it has broadcasting capability;

2. It is independent of distance; and

3. It can handle multi-media documents (e.g., numbers, text, graphics, music, voice, sound, and image).[10]

The configuration of the satellite system includes a personal computer (a telephone and facsimile machine can also be included) linked to a system control center which, in turn, is linked to the outdoor VSAT. The VSAT either sends information to or receives it from the satellite, which has received it from the central site, or hub earth stations.[11]

On-Line Information Systems
On-Line Data Bases

On-line data base services are a standard resource in most special libraries. These data bases can provide the special librarian with unique information in almost any field. Libraries are turning more frequently to on-line services rather than having expensive subscriptions to journals, abstracts, and indexes.

There is an increasing trend among U.S. data base publishers to provide the full text of documents on-line. An article delivered on-line is not an exact reproduction of the original article. Typeface, layout, and graphics are not reproduced; only the text (the author's words) is preserved and delivered. The full-text data base is another

Figure 6.1. Computer equipment furniture, Texas Woman's University. Photograph courtesy of Metropolitan Business Systems, Inc.

way to expand the special library's collection without the allocation of additional space.

On-Line Catalogs and Circulation Systems

Any new special library should have an on-line catalog and circulation system. If an existing special library plans to move or renovate, those plans should include the installation of a computer-based cataloging, circulation, acquisition, and serials control system.

Hard copy catalogs can be converted to an on-line system, and a computer program can automate manual circulation and technical services operations. Programs for these purposes are available commercially as are basic data base packages customized for library applications. Software will require some modification to meet the differing needs of each library. Libraries can use a retrospective conversion facility to change from a hard copy catalog to an on-line system. Some libraries do not convert old catalogs to an on-line system; they simply start putting acquisitions on-line.

The on-line catalog should network with the organization's LANs and other information networks to which the special library belongs. Space should be allocated for the computer hardware, as well as for the furniture that houses it.

Microform Technology

Microform technology is the most traditional method used by libraries to conserve space, preserve materials, and increase collection size. It has been used in libraries for more than fifty years. Most information professionals are familiar with the advantages of microform technology, including space savings, speed and convenience of retrieval, security and preservation, fixed file continuity, easy reversion to paper, and the legal admissibility of microfilm records. Disadvantages include the lack of acceptance by patrons, cost, equipment constraints, and high conversion turnaround time.

The micrographics industry is attempting to overcome the disadvantages of its product and capitalize on its advantages. Updatable microfilm, colored microfilm, and better equipment are available. Similarly, computer output microfilm (COM) and computer-assisted retrieval (CAR) are two technologies which focus on microfilm's positive aspects.

Computer Output Microfilm (COM)

COM is the production of microfilm from computer-processed data. Computerized magnetic tape is transferred to 16mm or 35mm microfilm. The COM system has three major parts: the recording device; the interfacing, sequencing, and indexing device; and a printer that can be used to produce hard copy.[12]

COM can store enormous volumes of material in compact form. With COM, unwieldy computer printouts can be eliminated. Microfilm requires only one to twelve percent of the space of its paper counterpart. For information sharing, microfilm is less cumbersome than paper, especially with quantities of material. Accessing the information is simpler with microfilm, particularly through the use of a computer-assisted retrieval (CAR) unit.

CAR systems have not completely overcome the disadvantages of ordinary microfilm. For example, document clarity is not great, especially when compared with the excellent images produced by optical storage methods. COM has further disadvantages such as its exorbitant cost, inability to edit stored information, and unproven archivability of the microfilm itself.[13]

Computer-Assisted Retrieval (CAR)

CAR systems have several information management functions. CAR is most often applied to indexing, but is also used for locating and cross-referencing material. CAR is a computer-based index to microfilm images. It can be used on a mainframe, mini-, or microcomputer. A basic data base package can create the index, or the librarian can use CAR indexing software, although at much greater cost.

A CAR microform system used in the special library would consist of the microfilm storage device, an image retrieval system, computer terminals, a central processing unit, and software.[14] The system can have a telecommunications link to remote locations with telephone lines, cables, or satellites.

The primary benefits of CAR systems include fast and efficient retrieval of records, indexing, and cross-referencing applications; misfiling reductions; and report generation. CAR systems have the added advantage of over twenty-five years of availability. The

Figure 6.2. Microfiche storage equipment. Photograph courtesy of Metropolitan Business Systems, Inc.

Figure 6.3. Micrographics equipment, Texas Woman's University.
Photograph courtesy of Metropolitan Business Systems, Inc.

limitations of CAR include its high cost, limited access, and complex system design.[15]

Space Planning for Microfilm Technology

Because film is air-sensitive, microform storage space should have a controlled temperature of approximately 70 degrees F and a relative humidity of 40 to 50 percent. The microform should be protected from water and dust.

Film reels require one square foot of storage space for every 100 reels of 35mm film, 200 reels of 16mm, and 2300 fiche. Remember to provide space for the storage of such supplies as paper, bulbs, cleaners, and spare parts.[16]

Floor load capacity should be at least 170 pounds per square foot, compared with 150 pounds per square foot for the rest of the library.[17] When planning the space, consider growth and expansion because micrographic-based resources will also accumulate over the years.

Space allocation for the microform work area depends on the system and equipment selected. Select the equipment prior to planning the space so that it can be accommodated comfortably and efficiently in the overall library design. Reserve space next to the reader or reader/printer as a patron work area. The microform work area should be soundproofed to absorb machine and residual noise.

In-House Data Bases

A library may want to develop an in-house data base of specialized information which may not be commercially available. Data base software can produce an in-house data base, or, if the information is voluminous and will be distributed widely, it may be appropriate to produce CD-ROM.

If the information for the data base is not in digital form and only exists on paper or microform, you must convert the information to digital format. The documents can be entered into the computer by a data entry operator. Although accurate, this is costly and time consuming. An alternative is to use a scanner and convert the printed page to machine-readable form.

There are currently two types of scanning: optical character recognition (OCR) and image scanning. OCR software is used to scan standard type fonts, i.e., typewritten text. Image scanners will scan typeset text and graphics. The latter scanning method is used for graphics reproduction and desktop publishing applications.

The electronic special library makes unique demands on the architecture and interior design of the special library. Computer equipment requires a secure environment and adequate wiring for electric power and telecommunications services.

Most of the electronic information service offered by the special library will be microcomputer-based, namely, CD-ROM, on-line data bases, on-line catalogs, and optical disks. Each of these will require peripheral or telecommunications links. Planning for these technologies should include a degree of flexibility because technologies are upgraded frequently and older models may quickly become obsolete. Micrographics technology is less sensitive to sweeping technological innovations, but its roles as a traditional library storage device and collection enhancer could diminish as optical technology becomes more accessible and affordable. For a select bibliography of library technology sources, refer to Appendix 6.

NOTES

1. John Markoff, "The PC's Broad New Potential." *The New York Times* November 30, 1989, D1.

2. Ibid., D8.

3. Laura Buddine and Elizabeth Young, *The Brady Guide to CD-ROM* Simon and Schuster, Inc., New York, NY, 1987, 15.

4. Ibid., D8.

5. Patrick Honan, "What's New in Optical Storage," *Personal Computing* February, 1989, 117.

6. Ibid., 113.

7. Richard W. Boss, *Information Technology and Space Planning for Libraries and Information Centers* G. K. Hall & Co., Boston, MA, 1987, 68.

8. Calvin Sims, "Satellite Use by Business is Growing," *The New York Times* October 26, 1988, D1.

9. Bob Winfield, "Document Transfer by Satellite," *ASLIB Proceedings* Vol. 36, No. 4, April 1984, 178.

10. Carolyn G. Weaver, "Electronic Document Delivery," *Encyclopedia of Library and Information Science* Vol. 40, Supplement 5. Marcel Dekker, Inc., New York, NY, 55.

11. Sims, D1.

12. "Computer Output Microfilm (COM)," *The Records and Retrieval Report* November 1985, Vol. 1, No. 9, 138.

13. Ibid., 141.

14. Boss, 47-48.

15. "Computer Assisted Retrieval (CAR)," *The Records and Retrieval Report* December 1985, 153.

16. Boss, 48.

17. Boss, 52.

Chapter 7. Increasing Resource Sharing

PARTICIPATION IN LIBRARY and information networks and consortia enables libraries to expand their collections without allocating additional space. The desirability of the network approach is enhanced now by electronic technology.

The electronic library is a fact of life. Special library service is dependent on the technological support provided by computers, telecommunications systems, micrographic equipment, and audiovisual devices. This technology is the basis of improved networks and resource sharing programs now available to special libraries.

Networking has several advantages: increased and more timely access to a greater base of information for organization employees or other library patrons, and significant savings in acquisitions, administrative overhead, and work hours spent maintaining, sorting, disposing of, and storing the collection. There are two kinds of networks: internal networks that are part of an organization's operations, and external networks in which member libraries participate. All special libraries with sizable collections in their fields benefit from participation in regional and national data bases.

Establishing the Network

Sharing collections saves space and increases resources. Collections are shared through either existing interlibrary loan (ILL) programs in a specialized industry or through the creation of new interlibrary loan projects. Loan programs permit the availability of increased resources, particularly journals, periodicals, and newspaper articles, which are especially suitable for ILL programs. Collection development can be planned to complement, rather than duplicate, the resources of member libraries.

Planning for the ILL or other resource-sharing programs can occur within the trade or professional association itself, or within the industry action committees of library and information science associations. Because their collections are comprehensive and current, independent special libraries might be the focal points for developing ILL programs with other libraries.

Cooperation is imperative in establishing networks, and there should be a strong commitment to planning and managing the network. Agree on subject areas and priorities. Establish standards, particularly with computer hardware and software, in order to achieve compatibility for data transfer. There should be some flexibility for upgrading the technology and the resources, introducing new products, and changing the collection to reflect shifting business trends.

Interlibrary Loan (ILL)

The growing sophistication of information technology has expanded the options that libraries and information centers have for sharing resources. Interlibrary loan traditionally has not played a vital role in the dissemination of information because a typical ILL transaction is slow. A three-to five-day delivery time (via surface mail) is inappropriate in a financial or medical library or any other organization where vital information is required immediately. The potential of the ILL program is now being realized because of dramatic improvements to existing products and the development of new products for information transfer.

Technology for Resource Sharing

Several new technologies have been developed and tested for use in library resource-sharing programs. Some of these technologies have greater potential for the immediate future than others. The technologies discussed in this Chapter are telefacsimile, electronic mail, and local area networks.

Telefacsimile (FAX)

FAX is the process of transmitting printed and graphic documents over telephone lines. Although libraries have been using FAX machines for more than forty years, there was little satisfaction with its performance. Transmission was slow (about four and one-half to six minutes per page), the process was labor intensive, and document clarity was poor. Facsimile has come to the forefront of the new technologies largely because it involves little capital investment and is installed and maintained easily. FAX costs less than courier and overnight mail services and gets the information or document to its destination more quickly.

Compatibility problems between different brands of facsimile machines were resolved in 1981 when the telefacsimile industry adopted an international standard. Under this standard, Group 3 machines are compatible with other Group 3 FAX machines, as well as with the older Group 1 and Group 2 FAXes. Group 4 FAX machines, which are being marketed now in Germany, have a transmission speed of three to five seconds per page, resulting in lower transmission costs.[1]

Currently, digital FAX equipment can transmit a page in fifteen to sixty seconds, while significantly improving document clarity. An automatic document feeder facilitates the transmission of multipage documents. Page feeders are a standard FAX option, although the number of pages they hold varies.

A FAX network with other frequently contacted libraries or organizations (or a special library with satellite collections) is more advantageous than an independent installation because it allows for standardization of equipment and transmission procedures, as well as for reduced costs.

Dedicated FAX Networks

Traditionally, FAX machines have been carried over telecommunications voice networks (standard telephone lines). To sidestep the competition for telecommunications space between phone messages and FAX messages, a dedicated FAX network was introduced in late 1988 by MCI Communications. The service, called MCI Fax, is a dedicated network that transmits FAX documents over fiber-optic lines. With a digital connection, transmission speeds are faster, and image quality is better than with voice communications. The MCI Fax includes customized dialing plans, 800-line service, delivery confirmation, and distribution and security control features, among other services. The network accommodates all types of FAX equipment, and other machines, such as telex, electronic mail, and personal computers, can be used to send FAX documents.

Costs are lower on dedicated FAX networks because billing is for the actual time used. On voice transmission lines, billing is done in one-minute increments. Dedicated FAX networks are particularly advantageous to special libraries with heavy FAX volumes, such as law and medical libraries.[2]

Stand-Alone versus PC-FAX

A FAX machine can be either a stand-alone unit or a personal computer equipped with a FAX board (PC-FAX). Although both types will transmit printed and graphic documents similarly, there are differences.

The stand-alone FAX hardware includes a scanner, modem, and telephone. Some FAXes are multipurpose; they are configured as a photocopier, telephone answering machine, and printer for dedicated word processors and personal computers. For the latter, the FAX must be equipped with communications software.

A personal computer can double as a FAX machine when a FAX board is installed. Only computer-generated data can be sent via the PC-FAX, an advantage to the special librarian who can send the results of an on-line data base query directly to the requestor's computer file. Hard copy documents can not be transmitted with a PC-FAX unless the document is first scanned into the FAX format. The personal computer should be equipped with a high-quality printer (e.g., a laser or inkjet) if a hard copy of the FAX document is required. FAX documents are not read by the printer as text documents, but rather as picture files. The decoding of the picture file by the printer can take a considerable amount of time. PC-FAX messages can be downloaded to the word processing package with intelligent character recognition (ICR) software.

Accessibility to the FAX is more limited with a PC-FAX configuration than with the stand-alone machine. Generally, a stand-alone FAX is used by many people; personal computers usually are used by one person, thus limiting access to the FAX function.

Some PC-FAX packages allow the computer's use for word processing, data base, and other applications, even when the PC-FAX mode is operating. With PC-FAX, the computer receives the document and a screen prompt or mailbox message alerts the addressee. If the PC-FAX is unable to accept FAXes "in the background," use of the personal computer for other work is severely restricted.[3]

Space Planning Considerations

The stand-alone FAX is small and easy to install. Place it in an area of the library where it is accessible to patrons and staff, but will not interfere with research or other work requiring a noise-free environment. Electric power and telephone lines should be nearby.

Electronic Mail (E-Mail)

Electronic mail is the delivery of messages from one terminal to another through a host computer. It is becoming an integral part of communications systems. In libraries, E-mail is used for interlibrary loan, document delivery, and general communications as well as the library's on-line catalog.[4]

There are two types of E-mail: locally-oriented systems within the physical confines of the organization that houses the computer, and geographically diverse systems which are served by commercial and public E-mail systems. A closed but commercial E-mail system is also available for organizations that need to communicate with branch offices or other remote installations.

A public system provides access to on-line data bases worldwide, and vital research information can be obtained quickly. A requested document can be delivered electronically, or a hard copy can be obtained via surface mail or courier service.

Assisting with research services is just one of E-mail's functions in the special library. E-mail and the on-line catalog can be linked to transmit bibliographic records, using the machine-readable cataloging (MARC) format. E-mail can alert users to recent acquisitions to the collection, a selective dissemination of information (SDI) function. Yet another function is the use of a template for creating and transmitting bibliographic records in ILL transactions. E-mail allows users to make specific requests, to suggest new acquisitions, or to check the status of a reserved item. E-mail service can be used to eliminate many of the clerical and paper-intensive tasks required by the library's technical services operations.

Incompatibility is a problem with today's E-mail. Unlike the telefacsimile industry, efforts towards E-mail standardization are not progressing quickly. Most E-mail compatibility problems are related to the address, text, and tracking codes, which are different within each service. A uniform code for each address would be created by an international standard, thus allowing global exchange of information.

Local Area Networks (LAN)

The special library or information center can increase accessibility to its resources with a local area network (LAN). Text, graphics, and audio and video can be distributed through the LAN. A LAN can provide access to the on-line catalog, data bases, engineering and architectural drawings, and any other resources stored on CD-ROM or other optical storage media. Peripherals can also be linked and shared by the network.

Transmission Media

The LAN does not use external telephone lines or any other commercial telecommunication systems for its communications. The most common cabling for LANs are twisted pair, shielded wire, and fiber optics.

Twisted pair is most economical for applications that do not require high speed and/or great distance. Shielded coaxial cable provides higher transmission speeds over longer distances than does twisted pair. However, it is unwieldy and expensive to install. Fiber optic cable is constructed from glass, and light pulses transmit the signals. The advantages of fiber optic cable are very high transmission speeds, no electro-magnetic interference, high security, and easy installation. The disadvantage is cost because of the need for expensive interfaces.

LAN Configurations

There are four major types of network configurations: star, bus, tree, and ring. The star configuration connects terminals (either dumb or intelligent) to a centralized computer. The central network file server feeds the data to the central computer. The bus configuration connects all computers directly to the main cable line. Signals are sent along the line, and the targeted addresses will accept messages from the sender. Data meant for one address will bypass the nontargeted addresses.[5]

Computers are hooked to file servers that disseminate the data. The ring configuration is the fourth type of LAN. It is a circle of cable to which the terminals are linked. Signals are passed around the ring and accepted by a computer when the signal is recognized. Otherwise, the signal bypasses the terminal and moves to the next one.

Space Planning for the LAN

The installation of LANs is becoming more commonplace, and many organizations are including the library or information center on the network. When installing the LAN, pay attention to the building and its interior design. Wiring is an important consideration because the LAN will require extensive cabling that could be affected by the building's architecture. For example, older buildings might have solid walls, meaning the cable should be run on the outside of the wall.

Other considerations concerning cable installation include existing cable and its location, local fire regulations for wire shielding, and the type of cable for the LAN being installed. LAN terminals should have convenient electrical outlets, and there should be appropriate space for the terminals.

Traditional Library Networks and Consortia

State and regional networks generally serve the interests of public libraries, although some "public" networks accommodate special subject interest. For example, the major network for health sciences libraries in the United States is the Regional Medical Library Network coordinated by the National Library of Medicine. This network provides the on-line service called Medical Literature Analysis and Retrieval System (MEDLARS).[6]

Because of competition within their industry, special libraries might consider their resources and information proprietary and might be inclined not to join or establish consortia. However, for an industry which requires diverse and extensive research information, participation in a consortia could eliminate the need for libraries to house similar types of information.

Many special libraries in the New York City area are members of the New York Metropolitan Reference and Research Library Agency (METRO). Members include the Engineering Societies Library, Metropolitan Museum Library, and New York Zoological Society Library. According to its charter, METRO makes "the best use of already available resources through cooperative efforts and, in the same manner, builds additional resources when appropriate." METRO focuses on advanced information resources and services which public libraries cannot always provide. METRO estimates that its libraries contain "75 percent of New York state's research materials" and serve "48 percent of the users of research materials."[7]

Special libraries participate in other library consortia across the country. Some industries provide information networks, albeit informal, to industry organizations. For example, the textile industry sponsors the Textile Information Users Council, which is a loosely structured textile information network.[8]

Bibliographic Utilities and Service Centers

Bibliographic network systems offer technical services support to special libraries through such providers as the On-Line Computer

Library Center (OCLC), Research Libraries Information Network (RLIN), and University of Toronto Library Automation Services (Utlas). All the bibliographic data is derived from MARC tapes developed by the Library of Congress.

On-Line Computer Library Center (OCLC)
OCLC offers special libraries shared cataloging, serials control, on-line union catalog, on-line reference, interlibrary loan, and retrospective conversion of manual records into machine readable form. User groups have been formed within particular industries for the benefit of OCLC participants and are sometimes affiliated with a professional association.[9]

Research Libraries Information Network (RLIN)
RLIN is a bibliographic utility operated by the Research Libraries Group, a corporation with thirty-three member libraries. RLIN is targeted at research and academic libraries and uses MARC tapes as the basis of its services. RLIN is more subject-oriented than OCLC, thus offering an advantage to special libraries. It provides specialized data bases for the art and geography fields.

University of Toronto Library Automation System (UTLAS)
Utlas is another bibliographic utility offering cataloging, acquisition, interlibrary loan, computer output microfilm (COM) catalogs, acquisition lists, magnetic tapes, and catalog cards.

Smaller, regional-based networks, also called service centers, exist across the country and provide retrospective conversion services, microfilm catalogs, on-line searching, hardware, electronic mail services, serials control, and data base management. Some of these service centers include the Capital Consortium Network (CAPCOM) in Washington, D.C.; Federal Library and Information Network (FEDLINK), also in Washington; New England Library and Information Network (NELINET), based in Newton, Massachusetts; and Minnesota Interlibrary Telecommunication Exchange (MINITEX), from Minneapolis.
Whether designing a new library or upgrading or expanding an existing one, you should plan to participate in networks. The

networks will enable the special library to expand its collection without requiring additional space. Traditional library networks and consortia are useful. However, electronically based networks using state-of-the-art technologies should be a priority. FAX networks and LAN offer the most data transfer potential for the immediate future. Emerging technologies such as satellite systems and video text and disks, will also make contributions to resource sharing in libraries. When designing the new special library, provide adequate space using these technologies. A list of references to help your resource sharing efforts is provided in Appendix 7.

NOTES

1. G. Gordon Long, "Fax Growth Hinges on Needs of Users," *Office Systems 88,* September, 50.

2. Calvin Sims, "MCI Plans a Separate Facsimile Network," *The New York Times* November 4, 1988, D1, D6.

3. Peter H. Lewis, "Fax Machines and Modems: Who Needs Which?", *The New York Times* February 21, 1989, C13.

4. Eben L. Kent, "Electronic Mail," *Encyclopedia of Library and Information Science* Vol. 40, Supplement 5, Marcel Dekker, Inc., New York, 1986, 64.

5. Ibid., 35-36.

6. James F. Williams, II, "The Special Library's Role in Networks: A MEDLARS Perspective," *The Special Library Role In Networks* Special Libraries Association, New York, 1980, 185.

7. Forrest F. Carhart, "Metro and Special Libraries," *The Special Library Role In Networks* Special Libraries Association, New York, 1980, 95.

8. Georgia H. Rodeffer, "Textile Information Users Council and Information Transfer in the Textile Industry," *The Special Library Role In Networks* Special Libraries Association, New York, 1980, 57.

9. Mary Ellen L. Jacob, "Special Libraries and OCLC," *The Special Library Role In Networks* Special Libraries Association, New York, 1980, 155.

Appendixes

Appendix 1. Collection and Collection Housing Measurement Forms

Form for Equipment and Furniture Inventory/ Measurement

TYPE OF EQUIPMENT/FURNITURE_____ _____

LOCATION _____

HEIGHT _____ WIDTH _____ DEPTH _____

USE _____

BOOK STOCK _____ NONBOOK STOCK _____

RANGE NUMBER _____   MICROFILM _____

SECTION NUMBER _____   MICROFICHE_____

COLLECTION MEASUREMENT   APERTURE CARD _____

(LFF OR LFI) _____   8MM FILM _____

    16MM FILM _____

START CALL NUMBER _____   35MM FILM _____

END CALL NUMBER _____   SLIDES _____

    VERTICAL FILES _____

    CD-ROM _____

    VIDEOTAPES _____

    DISKETTES _____

    VIDEOCASSETTES _____

    RECORDS _____

    AUDIOCASSETTES_____

    OTHER _____

CALL NUMBER/COLLECTION RANGE _____

NUMBER OF SHELVES/DRAWERS _____

NOTES _____

ANALYST/S _____

DATE _____

FORM FOR COLLECTION MEASUREMENT - NONBOOK STOCK

COLLECTION MEASUREMENT-NONBOOK STOCK   LOCATION_____

TYPE OF CABINET_____

_____MICROFILM   8 mm FILM_____

_____MICROFICHE   16 mm FILM_____

_____APERTURE CARD   35 mm FILM_____

_____VERTICAL FILES   CD-ROM_____

_____VIDEOTAPES   DISKETTES_____

_____VIDEOCASSETTES   RECORDS_____

_____SLIDES   AUDIOCASSETTES_____

                                    OTHER_____

CALL NUMBER/COLLECTION RANGE_____

NUMBER OF SHELVES/DRAWERS_____

COLLECTION MEASUREMENT (LFF or LFI)_____

NOTES_____

     _____

ANALYST/S_____

DATE_____

FORM FOR COLLECTION MEASUREMENT - BOOK STOCK

COLLECTION MEASUREMENT-BOOK STOCK   LOCATION_____

RANGE NUMBER_____   SECTION NUMBER_____

COLLECTION MEASUREMENT (LFF or LFI)_____

START CALL NUMBER_____   END CALL NUMBER_____

NOTES_____

_____

ANALYST/S_____

DATE_____

Appendix 2. Questions to Ask Before Doing Layout

1. What are all the separately housed collection holdings? Determine present linear inches/feet for each of these. Keep in mind that a shelf is considered to be full when it is actually three quarters full. This is to allow for easy access and for expansion space. If shelves are at full capacity, it is advisable to increase their number by 25 percent. Investigate microfilming, or consider high-density mobile equipment.

2. Do materials in circulation also have to be considered?

3. Are there plans for extensive weeding of the collection?

4. What is the net growth rate of each collection element? Project the estimated growth rate and determine the number of additional linear inches/feet needed.

5. Identify current storage equipment. Would a change in type of equipment or additional equipment be better?

6. What is the total number of staff members?

7. What is the desirable traffic and what is the work flow? Determine groupings of workstations and work areas and user reference areas.

8. What equipment is necessary in each area? What space is required? What electrical outlets are necessary?

9. How can work and reference areas be arranged to provide the most effective work flow and the most desirable traffic lanes?

10. Is work done in two or more areas so closely related that they should be considered one area?

11. Does staff work require the use of tools that are also available to library users (e.g., indexes, computer terminals, microfilm/fiche equipment)? If so, is this area accessible to users?

12. Will the entrance to the reading/reviewing area have good traffic flow and a hospitable appearance?

13. Are there security requirements?

14. Can there be adequate visual supervision of entrances and exits?

15. Does the allocated space include supporting columns that may introduce problems? What about the shape of the space itself?

16. Can columns be incorporated into shelf range? It is uneconomical to have any fill-in shelving section less than twenty-four inches wide.

17. If wall shelving is to be used, are there unbroken wall areas that will allow maximum use of shelving?

18. Are walls able to support shelving or other equipment attached to them?

19. Will the location of windows, doors, heating and air-conditioning units, and electrical outlets create any problems in the placement of shelves or other equipment? For example, the location of doors may determine the traffic

flow and the direction of their swing may affect the placement of equipment.

20. Will the height or size of windows or the direction they face allow direct sunlight which will create glare and harm documents?

21. Are lighting and ventilation adequate?

22. Can aisles be designed so space on each side can be used?

Appendix 3. Preplanning the Library

The Library's Role in the Organization

1. Does the library serve individuals or groups outside the organization?

2. Does it serve the whole organization or was it established to provide service for particular departments or offices?

3. If this library does not serve the whole organization, what other library or information facilities are available within the organization?

4. Does the inaccessibility or lack of other library services require this library to serve a larger group than would be supposed and to what extent and in what way are these additional people serviced?

5. Analyze the group that the library is expected to serve in terms of the following:

   a. Size.

   b. What are the general library requirements of this group in terms of service and type and extent of library collections?

   c. To what extent is the library able to meet these requirements?

   d. What are the developing library needs of this group? Are they toward expansion and intensification of existing services or toward greater diversification and addition of new services? Are there services that can or may soon be dropped?

   e. How adequately does the library collection meet the present requirements made of it (e.g., specific subject fields that require strengthening or re-placement)?

6. Considering the company's potential development and the developing needs of the group that the library serves, what are the long range possibilities of its library?

7. On the same basis, what are the short term possibilities that must be considered for the period for which the new library area is being planned?

8. In preparing for the immediate and short term needs, are you building into your plan any factors that may later become handicaps toward future development?

9. Can other information facilities within the organization be incorporated into this library in the future? Will your plans make this possible?

10. If the library was established to serve only a portion of the organization, and there is a possibility that future development may require it to serve all or a larger section of the organization, the potential requirements of these additional library users should also be considered.

11. Are special equipment and service requirements emerging (e.g., computers, microfilm and microfiche readers, storage of microfilm and microfiche, photographic reproduction equipment, CD-ROM, AV equipment, etc.)?

12. Does the library hold any subscriptions to on-line data bases? Does it have or is it contemplating automated catalog or circulation and routing systems?

General Description of Present and Planned Library

1. List the services the library currently performs. This would include the acquisition of published material (for the library collection and perhaps also for other departments of the company); the organization of library materi-

als by cataloging and classification, vertical subject files, etc.; routing of periodicals; reference works; literature searches; bulletins and abstracting publications of the library.

2.   Make a list of any new services to be performed in the planned library as well as any services that will be discontinued.

Library Staff

1.   What is the number of professional and nonprofessional staff members?

2.   What employment number is planned for the new library?

3.   Develop a detailed job description, with time allotments for each duty performed. This will later be related to the equipment required and to the layout of work areas.

Visits to Other Libraries

Visit other libraries:

1.   To discover both good and bad ideas.

2.   To evaluate the usefulness of equipment planned for purchase.

3.   To test ideas of design and layout against their practical functioning in libraries where they may have been incorporated and to develop new ideas.

4.   To examine the equipment and layout of general office areas, file rooms, etc., for additional ideas.

  Reprinted with permission from Metropolitan Business Systems, Inc.

Appendix 4. Space Planning Statistics and Standards

For estimating purposes in a special library, a single-faced section of steel shelving is considered to hold 125 to 150 books. For a more detailed estimate in a book collection that is fairly uniform in size, an estimate of 6 to 7 books per linear foot and 5 reference books per linear foot is used. Bound periodicals average 4 to 5 volumes per linear foot.

In relation to aisles, free-standing shelving ranges which do not exceed 18 feet (6 sections) are recommended as a general standard. If the ranges are on dead-end aisles, they should be shorter by at least one shelving section.

The height of the book stack must allow at least 18 inches clearance from the top of the stack to the bottom of the overhead sprinkler to comply with fire code regulations.

Suggested Space Standards

Aisles
Center or main aisles: 4' - 4½'
Between tables and walls: 5'
Between tables, if chairs are back to back: 5' - 6'
Between single tables: 4'
Between table ends without chairs: 3½' - 4'
Between files, if facing: 6'
Between bookstacks and between bookstacks and wall shelving: 30"- 3' (4' - 4½' is preferable for moderate or heavy use to permit through traffic and book carts)

Areas
In front of circulation desk: 6'
In front of card catalog: 5'
In front of reference desk: 5' - 6'

Reading Room
75 sq. ft. per reader; if intensive research, this should be increased.

Staff
50 sq. ft. is the minimum per staff member. The recommended standard is 100 to 125 sq. ft. per staff member; 150 sq. ft. per staff member in technical processing. This includes for each staff member the desk, chair, filing cases, other equipment, and space around the desk that is required when consulting with other people. At least 225 sq. ft. should be allocated per administrative staff member.

Steel Shelving
Bracket shelving is available in the following standard measurements: heights are 90", 60", and 42". These heights include a base, which serves as the bottom shelf (3" to 4" high), a canopy top (2" - 2½" high), and shelves of approximately ¾". Widths are approximately 36".

Depths are expressed in "nominal" sizes: this is one inch deeper than the actual depth of the shelf because it is measured from the front face of the shelf to the center of the supporting column.

Most manufacturers now supply nominal 8", 9", 10", and 12" with still deeper shelves available for storage of folios, newspapers, etc. Ninety-inch high steel shelving is usually offered with 6 to 7 adjustable shelves.

The following measures apply to 90" shelving with a top canopy:

Six adjustable shelves plus the base provides 7 shelving spaces approximately 11" in height. The bottom edge of any book placed on the top shelf will be 76" from the floor.

Five adjustable shelves plus the base provides 6 shelving spaces of approximately 13" in height.

A double-faced steel shelving section with seven shelves on each side weighs approximately 800 to 900 pounds including books.

Wood Shelving
The standard heights for book shelving are 82", 60", and 42". This measure includes a base (4" high), a canopy top (2" to $2\frac{1}{2}$" high) and adjustable shelves approximately $\frac{3}{4}$" thick. The interior measure of an 82" standard unit is $75\frac{1}{2}$" with 69 adjustment holes set at 1" intervals.

Six adjustable shelves plus the base provides 7 shelving spaces ranging in height from $10\frac{1}{4}$" to just under 10".

Five adjustable shelves plus the base provides 6 shelving spaces ranging from $12\frac{1}{4}$" to just under 11".

The recommended standard shelf depth of wood shelving for library use is 10" (actual measure).

A double-faced wood shelving section with 7 shelves on each side weighs 725 pounds including books.

User Area
If it is necessary to seat more than one reader at a table, 36" is the recommended minimum table space per reader. A standard 4' x 6' table will seat four people.

Each reading space for microform users should be a minimum of 2' deep x 4' wide, but 3' x 5' is preferable. In planning, allow 40 sq. ft. per reading station.

Storage
Stationary book stack areas with ranges 7 shelves high placed 4'6" from center to center will yield 15.56 volumes per sq. foot. Mobile bookstack area with 7-shelf high ranges will yield 38.92 volumes per square foot (aisle space not included).

A cardboard box $8\frac{3}{8}$" x $10\frac{3}{4}$" x $4\frac{1}{8}$ will hold 12 rolls of 35mm film.

A fiberboard box 10" x 4" x 4" (inside dimensions) which opens on the long side with a hinged top will hold 6 microfilm reels.

A small, 3-section steel drawer holds 69 boxes of 16mm or 42 boxes of 35mm film.

A typical cabinet of 9 drawers, 4 compartments each, with a total size of 52" x $20\frac{1}{4}$" x $28\frac{1}{2}$", will house 100 reels of 16mm or 68 reels of 35mm film per drawer.

Maximum microfiche storage is 100 fiche per inch. A 2-drawer steel cabinet, $16\frac{1}{4}$" x $14\frac{5}{8}$" x $6\frac{3}{8}$", will hold 2,000 to 2,250 microfiche (14.8 x 10.5 cm).

The average card catalog drawer holds 1,000 usable cards. If use of the catalog is heavy, cases should be no more than 10 drawers high.

Sloped or hinged periodical display equipment will hold 3 periodicals per shelf. The average growth rate for periodicals is 7" per title per year.

Maximum storage of slides is 20 slides per inch.

Appendix 5. Computer Assisted Design (CAD) Software

1. Generic CAD by Generic Software, Inc.

2. DRAFIX CAD by Foresight Resources Corp. (also DRAFIX CAD ULTRA)

3. EasyCAD by Evolution Computing

4. DESIGNCAD by American Small Business Computers, Inc.

5. LaserCAD by American International Systems, Inc.

6. AUTOCAD by AUTODESK, Inc.

7. VERSACAD by T&W Systems, Inc.

8. CADVANCE by ISICAD, Inc.

Appendix 6. Select Library Technology References

Barrett, Robert. Digital Optical Disk Systems: A Review of Developments. The Future of Industrial Information Services, Library Association Industrial Group. 70-75. London: Taylor Graham, 1987.

Boss, Richard W. *Information Technologies and Space Planning for Special Libraries and Information Centers*. Boston: G.K. Hall & Co., 1987.

Buddine, Laura, and Elizabeth Young. *The Brady Guide to CD-ROM*. New York: Simon & Schuster, 1987.

"Computer Assisted Retrieval (CAR)." *The Records and Retrieval Report* 1, no. 10 (December 1985).

"Computer Output Microfilm (COM)." *The Records and Retrieval Report* 1, no. 9 (November 1985): 137-142.

De Gennaro, Richard. *Libraries, Technology and the Information Marketplace*. Boston: G.K. Hall & Co., 1987.

"Designing Library Facilities for a High Tech Future." *Library High Technology* (Winter 1987): 103-109.

Honan, Patrick. "What's New in Optical Storage." *Personal Computing* (February 1989): 111-118.

Markoff, John. "The PC's Broad New Potential." *The New York Times* (November 30, 1988): D1, D8.

Michaels, David Leroy. "Technology's Impact on Library Interior Planning." *Library High Technology,* (Winter 1987): 59-63.

O'Malley, Christopher. "What's New in Scanning." *Personal Computing* (March 1989): 103-110.

"Optical Character Recognition." *The Records and Retrieval Report* 3 no. 2 (February 1987): 1-10.

"Optical Memory Systems 1989." *The Records and Retrieval Report* 5 no. 2 (February 1989): 1-12.

Robinson, Phillip. "The Paper Chase." *PC/Computing* (November 1988): 164-179.

Saffady, William. "Advanced Records Management: Automated Document Storage, Control, and Retrieval Systems." Course at George Washington University, Washington, D.C., March 30-31, 1989.

— — —. *Optical Storage Technology 1988: A State of the Art Review.* Westport, Ct.: Meckler, 1988.

Sims, Calvin. "Satellite Use By Business is Growing." *The New York Times* (October 26, 1988): D8.

Weaver, Carolyn G. "Electronic Document Delivery." In vol. 40, supp. 5 of *Encyclopedia of Library and Information Science.* New York: Marcel Dekker, 1986.

Winfield, Bob. "Document Transfer by Satellite." ASLIB Proceedings 36, no. 4 (April 1984): 177-185.

Appendix 7. Increasing Resource Sharing References

Brilliantine, Lance R. "Design and Selection Guide to Local Area Networks." *Administrative Management* (October 1989): 34-38.

Buckland, Michael K. "Combining Electronic Mail With Online Retrieval in a Library Context." *Information Technology and Libraries* (December 1987): 266-271.

Finlay, Douglas. "Facsimile and Electronic Mail: Proving Better Accuracy and Speed for Tighter Communications." *Administrative Management* (November 1986): 17-22.

Kent, Eben L. "Electronic Mail." In *Encyclopedia of Library and Information Science* 40, supp. 5. New York: Marcel Dekker: 1986.

Lewis, Peter H. "The Facts on the Fax." *New York Times* (January 10, 1989): C3.

— — —. "New Fax Machines: Getting More for Less." *New York Times* (January 17, 1989): C6.

Long, G. Gordon. "Fax Growth Hinges on Needs of Users." *Office Systems 88* (September): 43, 46, 48, 50.

"The Role of the Special Library in Networks and Cooperatives: Executive Summary and Recommendations." Special Libraries Association, National Commission on Libraries and Information Science/SLA Task Force, New York, 1984.

Sims, Calvin. "MCI Plans a Separate Facsimile Network." *New York Times* (November 4, 1988): D1, D6.

"The Special Library Role in Networks." Robert W. Gibson, Jr., Ed., Special Libraries Association. New York: 1980.

Appendix 8. Selected Space Planning Terms

Anthropometrics: The study of human body measurements for the correct scaling of sizes, heights, and shapes of furniture and equipment.

Arc reach: The area covered by the swing of an arm.

Biomechanics: The study of the musculoskeletal effort of human beings to minimize work strain.

Blueprint: A photographic reproduction of architectural or engineering plans in black or white on a blue background.

CAR (computer-assisted retrieval): The use of a computer to assist in locating a record within a microform (i.e., microfilm, microfiche, ultrafiche) or computer-based system. In the microfilm field, CAR is often a fully automated retrieval system.

CD-ROM (compact disk-read only memory): A form of optical storage that distributes large amounts of digital information to users. The data on the disk is prerecorded and can not be erased or edited.

Central square concept: Special areas are set aside in a square configuration as the focal point from which all activities radiate or converge, i.e., the heaviest user activities.

Computer-aided design (CAD): The interface of computers and special software to produce architectural drawings enabling the space planner to easily move structural components, furniture, and equipment around on the screen.

COM (computer output microfilm): The recording of information that has been computer processed and is the end product of the computer operation, on microfilm. With the advance of the computer, microfilm readers were developed that photograph images from the display monitor or that record electronic beams directly from the computer. A form of converting computer-generated data into usable information on microfilm.

Configuration loss: The unavoidable loss of usable space because of unassignable space in an area.

Dead load: The weight of the building itself, e.g., steel, concrete, and wood components of the building.

Diffused light: Scattered light.

Electronic mail (E-mail): The transmission of messages from one terminal to another through a host computer.

Ergonomics: The relationship of humans to their working environment.

Floor load capacity: The weight that the floor can structurally support.

Floor plan: An architectural scale drawing, showing the size and arrangement of rooms, halls, equipment, and other items on one floor of a building.

Footcandle: A unit of light measure that approximates the light of a candle one foot from its flame.

High-density mobile shelving: A system of movable shelving units that run on tracks increasing storage capacity over conventional storage methods such as cabinets or stationary shelving, and allowing more units per square foot with fewer aisles.

Light spill: The configuration of light once it leaves the bulb or fixture.

Linear measurement: The measurement of books or files to determine how much material is housed in a particular facility.

Live load: The weight of items or people that move or can be moved around the building, e.g., books, equipment, supplies, fixtures, furniture, and people.

Local area network (LAN): The distribution of information services to a number of terminals using cables rather than external telephone lines or commercial telecommunications systems.

Motion economy: The concept of saving energy and eliminating unnecessary motions.

Nonassignable space: Space that cannot be used, e.g., corridors, stairwells, elevators, rest rooms, mechanical rooms, nonusable nooks and crannies.

Optical disk: A high-density random-access device that uses laser light (i.e., a laser beam) to store and read data and images at high speeds.

Payload: The weight of the material to be housed on the shelves.

PC-Fax: A system in which computer text and graphic documents in electronic format are converted to FAX format and are transmitted directly from the personal computer (PC) through the use of a PC-FAX board with a built-in, high-speed modem and FAX software.

Scanner: A device that scans printed, typed, or handwritten text, drawings, and photographs and automatically transmits the data to a work or data processing device, or stores the data in digital form on a computer storage medium.

Space planning: The consideration of office space, arrangement of equipment, furniture and reference areas, work stations, environment, work flow, and the principles of motion economy when designing space.

Telefacsimile (FAX): The process of transmitting printed and graphic documents over telephone lines.

Template: A predrawn equipment and/or furniture replica which can be moved around on the floor plan to evaluate possible arrangements.

Veiling reflection: A light source directly in front of, and above, a person's line of sight that will cause the light to bounce from a work surface into the person's eyes reducing the contrast between the background and the work surface.

WORM (write once read many): An optical storage device that permits the recording of information once which can not be erased or changed.

Index

Blueprints, 34-35
definition, 137

Bolstering (Structural
strengthening), 17-18

Bookcases
(see Book stacks, Shelving)

Book ranges
(see Shelving ranges)

Book stacks
illustration, 57
layout of, 26, 27
lighting for, 86-87
storage capacity, 131
weight of, 16-17
(see also Collection housing,
Shelving)

Books
formula for computing
weight of, 66-67
linear measurements of, 9, 26-27
(see also Collections, measuring
size of)

Building contractor, 2

Buildings,
multi-level, 39
renovation of, 2, 24
structure of, 26

Cabinets
file cabinets, 8
measurements of, 8, 9
locks for, 9
storage cabinets, 68

Cabling
fiber optics, 112-113
shielded wire, 112
twisted pair, 112

CAD
(see Computer-assisted design)

Call number range, growth
projections of, 12
(see also Shelf list)

CAR
(see Computer-assisted retrieval)

Card catalog, 68
illustration, 74

Carrels, 32, 42, 45, 79
illustration, 47, 48

CD-ROM, 94-96, 103
definition, 137
space requirements for, 42, 96

Ceilings, 18-19
fire codes, 18
height of, 18
effect on noise levels, 18
effect on heating and cooling, 18
lighting fixtures for, 19, 86-87
in space planning, 18, 27
sprinkler installation, 18-19

Center column, high-density storage
equipment, 52

Central square concept, 38
definition, 137

Chairs, 29, 32, 41-42, 78
(also see Seating)